Fit Franchise Revolution: Building Success in Health and Wellness

On the Cusp of Adulthood and Facing an Uncertain Future

Tony Bruno

Table Of Contents

Chapter 1: Introduction to the Fit Franchise Revolution — 2

Chapter 2: The Health and Fitness Landscape — 8

Chapter 3: Mobile Fitness Studios — 14

Chapter 4: Nutritional Meal Prep Services — 20

Chapter 5: Wellness Retreats and Getaway Franchises — 26

Chapter 6: Online Personal Training Platforms — 32

Chapter 7: Eco-Friendly Fitness Products — 38

Chapter 8: Mental Health and Wellness Coaching — 44

Chapter 9: Corporate Wellness Programs — 50

Chapter 10: Specialized Fitness Classes — 56

Chapter 11: Health-Focused Meal Delivery Franchises — 61

Chapter 12: Fitness Technology and Wearable Devices — 67

Chapter 13: Building a Successful Franchise — 73

Chapter 14: Marketing Your Health and Wellness Franchise — 79

Chapter 15: Future of the Fit Franchise Revolution — 85

Chapter 1: Introduction to the Fit Franchise Revolution

The Evolution of Health and Wellness Franchising

The evolution of health and wellness franchising has transformed significantly over the past few decades, driven by a growing awareness of fitness and well-being among the general population. Initially, the health and fitness industry was dominated by traditional gyms and fitness centers, which catered primarily to a niche audience. However, as lifestyle changes and health consciousness gained traction, a broader array of franchising opportunities emerged. This diversification has allowed entrepreneurs to tap into various niches, such as mobile fitness studios, nutritional meal prep services, and specialized fitness classes. The rise of technology has further propelled this evolution, giving birth to online personal training platforms and fitness apps that cater to consumers' changing preferences. One of the most notable trends in health and wellness franchising is the increased demand for convenience and flexibility. Busy lifestyles have prompted individuals to seek fitness solutions that fit seamlessly into their schedules. As a response, franchises such as mobile fitness studios have gained popularity, allowing trainers to bring workouts directly to clients' homes or workplaces. This model not only meets consumer needs but also provides entrepreneurs with lower overhead costs compared to traditional brick-and-mortar locations. The emphasis on convenience has also led to the rise of health-focused meal delivery franchises, which cater to those looking for nutritious meal options without the hassle of preparation. Another significant development in the health and wellness sector is the growing emphasis on holistic well-being. As consumers become more aware of the interconnectedness of physical, mental, and emotional health, franchises that offer comprehensive wellness solutions have flourished. Wellness retreats and getaway franchises have emerged as popular options for individuals seeking rejuvenation and self-care, while mental health and wellness coaching has gained prominence as a crucial component of overall health. This shift towards a more integrated approach to well-being has opened new avenues for entrepreneurs to create unique franchise concepts that address a wider range of consumer needs.

The incorporation of technology into health and wellness franchising has also played a pivotal role in its evolution. Fitness technology, including wearable devices and mobile applications, has revolutionized how consumers engage with their health. These innovations provide users with real-time data and personalized insights, empowering them to make informed decisions about their fitness journeys. As a result, franchises that leverage technology, such as online personal training platforms and fitness apps, have seen significant growth. This tech-driven approach not only enhances the consumer experience but also allows entrepreneurs to scale their businesses more effectively.

Lastly, the trend toward sustainability and eco-friendliness has begun to influence health and wellness franchising. As consumers increasingly prioritize environmental responsibility, franchises that focus on eco-friendly fitness products and sustainable practices are gaining traction. This shift reflects a broader cultural movement towards conscious consumption, where individuals are more discerning about the products and services they use. Entrepreneurs who align their franchise concepts with environmental values can attract a dedicated customer base, creating a competitive edge in the ever-evolving health and wellness landscape. Through understanding these trends, potential franchisees can strategically position themselves to thrive in this dynamic industry.

Why Franchising in the Wellness Sector?

Franchising in the wellness sector presents a unique opportunity for entrepreneurs looking to tap into a rapidly growing market. As consumers become more health-conscious, the demand for wellness services and products continues to rise. This trend creates a fertile ground for franchises that specialize in various aspects of health and wellness, including mobile fitness studios, nutritional meal prep services, and online personal training platforms. The appeal of franchising lies not only in the potential for profit but also in the ability to align business practices with a passion for health, making it an attractive option for many entrepreneurs.

One of the primary reasons to consider franchising in the wellness sector is the established business model that franchises provide. Entrepreneurs benefit from a proven framework that includes brand recognition, operational support, and marketing strategies. This reduces the risks typically associated with starting a new business from scratch. For instance, franchises in specialized fitness classes, such as yoga for seniors, come with a tried-and-true curriculum and established customer bases, which can lead to faster returns on investment and lower failure rates than independent ventures.

The wellness industry is characterized by its diverse niches, allowing franchisees to choose a path that resonates with their interests and expertise. Opportunities range from eco-friendly fitness products to wellness retreats and getaway franchises, catering to various consumer preferences. This diversity not only opens doors for entrepreneurs to find their niche but also enables them to address specific market demands. The flexibility within the wellness sector encourages innovation, allowing franchisees to adapt and expand their offerings to meet evolving client needs.

Moreover, the increasing focus on corporate wellness programs highlights the sector's potential for growth. Businesses are increasingly recognizing the importance of employee well-being, leading to a surge in demand for wellness solutions in the workplace. Franchises that offer tailored services, such as mental health and wellness coaching or fitness technology solutions, can capitalize on this trend. By integrating wellness into corporate environments, these franchises not only improve employee satisfaction and productivity but also create sustainable relationships with businesses, ensuring ongoing revenue streams.

Lastly, the wellness sector's alignment with societal values around health and sustainability enhances its appeal. Consumers are increasingly seeking brands that reflect their values, particularly in areas like eco-friendly fitness and health-focused meal delivery franchises. This alignment not only drives consumer loyalty but also positions wellness franchises as leaders in a movement that prioritizes holistic health. Entrepreneurs in this space have the opportunity to make a meaningful impact while building successful businesses that contribute positively to society, reinforcing why franchising in the wellness sector is a compelling choice.

Key Industry Trends

The health and wellness industry is undergoing a significant transformation as consumer preferences shift towards holistic approaches to well-being. One of the most notable trends is the rise of personalized health and fitness solutions. Entrepreneurs are increasingly leveraging technology to offer tailored experiences that cater to individual needs. This includes mobile fitness studios that provide on-demand workouts and nutritional meal prep services that create customized meal plans based on personal health goals. As consumers seek more individualized attention, franchises that prioritize personalization are likely to thrive in this competitive landscape.

Another key trend in the industry is the growing emphasis on mental health and wellness. The pandemic has highlighted the importance of mental well-being, prompting businesses to integrate mental health services into their offerings. Wellness retreats and getaway franchises are evolving to include programs focused on mental health, such as mindfulness workshops and stress management seminars. Similarly, mental health coaching is becoming an integral part of corporate wellness programs, as companies recognize the impact of mental health on employee productivity and satisfaction. This shift presents a lucrative opportunity for entrepreneurs who can effectively combine physical fitness with mental wellness solutions.

Sustainability is also shaping the direction of the health and wellness sector. Consumers are becoming increasingly aware of their environmental impact, leading to a demand for eco-friendly fitness products. Franchise models that offer sustainable equipment and apparel are gaining traction, appealing to environmentally conscious consumers. Additionally, health-focused meal delivery franchises are exploring eco-friendly packaging and sourcing practices, further aligning with this trend. Businesses that adopt sustainable practices not only meet consumer demand but also position themselves as responsible and forward-thinking in a crowded market.

The digital transformation of fitness is another pivotal trend influencing the industry. Online personal training platforms are becoming increasingly popular, allowing clients to access fitness coaching from the comfort of their homes. This shift is further accelerated by advancements in fitness technology and wearable devices that provide real-time feedback and analytics. Entrepreneurs who invest in digital solutions can reach a broader audience and enhance client engagement. As remote and hybrid fitness solutions become the norm, franchises that integrate technology into their services will be well-positioned for growth.

Lastly, the emergence of specialized fitness classes is reshaping the landscape of group fitness. Programs tailored for specific demographics, such as yoga for seniors or high-intensity workouts for busy professionals, are gaining popularity. This trend reflects a growing awareness of the diverse needs within the fitness community, encouraging entrepreneurs to create niche offerings that resonate with specific audiences. By focusing on specialized classes, franchise owners can differentiate themselves in a saturated market and build loyal customer bases. The future of the health and wellness industry lies in embracing these trends and adapting to the evolving preferences of consumers.

02

Chapter 2: The Health and Fitness Landscape

Overview of the Health and Fitness Industry

The health and fitness industry has evolved into a multifaceted sector that encompasses a wide array of services and products aimed at improving physical and mental well-being. With a growing awareness of health issues and lifestyle diseases, consumers are increasingly seeking solutions that not only enhance their fitness levels but also promote holistic wellness. This shift has resulted in a surge of opportunities for entrepreneurs and franchisees who are looking to capitalize on the rising demand for health-oriented services. From traditional gyms and fitness studios to innovative mobile fitness solutions, the landscape is constantly changing and expanding.

One of the most significant trends in the industry is the rise of specialized fitness classes and programs that cater to specific demographics. For instance, yoga for seniors, high-intensity interval training (HIIT), and prenatal fitness classes have gained traction as more individuals look for targeted solutions that suit their unique needs. These specialized offerings not only enhance client engagement but also allow franchise owners to differentiate themselves in a competitive market. The availability of niche fitness programs presents a lucrative opportunity for entrepreneurs to attract specific audiences while fostering a sense of community among participants.

In parallel, the popularity of nutritional meal prep services and health-focused meal delivery franchises is on the rise. As consumers become more conscious of their dietary choices, the demand for convenient, healthy meal options has surged significantly. This trend presents a unique opportunity for franchise businesses to provide tailored meal plans that cater to various dietary preferences and restrictions, such as vegan, gluten-free, or ketogenic diets. By integrating nutrition into their offerings, franchisees can create a comprehensive wellness experience that addresses both fitness and dietary needs, further enhancing customer loyalty and satisfaction.

Moreover, the advent of technology has dramatically transformed the health and fitness industry, paving the way for online personal training platforms and fitness technology products. Wearable devices and fitness apps have become essential tools for consumers seeking to track their progress and maintain accountability. Entrepreneurs have the opportunity to tap into this tech-driven aspect of the industry by creating innovative solutions that enhance user experience and promote healthy habits. The integration of technology not only provides additional revenue streams but also positions franchises as forward-thinking brands in a rapidly changing environment.

Finally, corporate wellness programs have emerged as a vital component of the health and fitness industry, with businesses increasingly recognizing the importance of employee well-being. By offering wellness initiatives, companies can reduce healthcare costs, improve employee morale, and enhance productivity. For franchise owners, this presents an opportunity to collaborate with organizations to provide tailored wellness solutions, ranging from on-site fitness classes to mental health coaching. By aligning franchise offerings with the needs of corporate clients, entrepreneurs can create sustainable, long-term partnerships that benefit both parties while contributing to a healthier workforce.

Emerging Niches in Health and Fitness

Emerging niches in health and fitness present exciting opportunities for entrepreneurs looking to capitalize on the growing consumer demand for wellness-oriented solutions. The rise of mobile fitness studios exemplifies this trend, offering convenience and flexibility for clients who prefer workouts outside traditional gym settings. These studios can cater to a variety of fitness levels and preferences, providing personalized experiences that appeal to busy professionals, families, and seniors. As the demand for on-the-go fitness solutions continues to grow, franchise models in this space can thrive, allowing entrepreneurs to tap into local markets with tailored offerings.

Nutritional meal prep services are another burgeoning niche that aligns with the health-conscious consumer's lifestyle. As people increasingly recognize the importance of proper nutrition in achieving fitness goals, meal prep franchises provide a convenient solution that saves time while ensuring healthy eating. By offering customizable meal plans that cater to specific dietary needs—such as vegan, gluten-free, or ketogenic—these services can attract a diverse clientele. Entrepreneurs can leverage local partnerships with farmers and nutritionists to enhance their offerings, creating a community-focused brand that resonates with health enthusiasts.

Wellness retreats and getaway franchises are gaining traction as people seek holistic approaches to health. These retreats often combine physical fitness, mental wellness, and nutritional education in serene environments, allowing participants to disconnect from daily stressors and reconnect with their health goals. Entrepreneurs can explore various themes, from yoga and meditation retreats to adventure-based fitness getaways, catering to niche markets such as corporate teams or wellness tourism. By creating immersive experiences that promote physical and mental rejuvenation, franchise owners can establish strong brand loyalty and attract repeat customers.

The rise of online personal training platforms has transformed the fitness landscape, offering entrepreneurs a chance to connect with clients digitally. With the ability to provide personalized training programs, nutrition advice, and ongoing support, these platforms cater to consumers who prefer working out at home or on their schedules. Entrepreneurs can differentiate their offerings through specialized niches, such as training for seniors, athletes, or busy professionals, while also integrating technology to enhance user experience through progress tracking and virtual coaching sessions.

Finally, the demand for eco-friendly fitness products is on the rise as consumers become increasingly aware of environmental issues. Entrepreneurs can capitalize on this trend by developing sustainable fitness gear, apparel, and accessories that appeal to eco-conscious consumers. Additionally, mental health and wellness coaching has emerged as a vital component of overall health, presenting opportunities for franchises focused on mindfulness practices, stress management, and emotional resilience. Corporate wellness programs that prioritize mental health can further establish a franchise's relevance in today's workplace, offering businesses valuable solutions to enhance employee well-being and productivity.

Importance of Adaptability in the Market

Adaptability is a critical factor for success in the competitive landscape of health and wellness franchises. As market dynamics shift rapidly due to technological advancements, changing consumer behaviors, and emerging trends, entrepreneurs must be able to pivot their strategies to meet evolving demands. This flexibility allows businesses to not only survive but thrive. For instance, as the popularity of mobile fitness studios has surged, franchises that quickly embraced this trend found themselves at the forefront of a lucrative market segment. By understanding the importance of adaptability, business leaders can position their franchises for long-term success.

In the realm of nutritional meal prep services, adaptability plays a significant role in addressing consumer preferences and dietary trends. As more individuals seek personalized nutrition plans, franchises that can quickly modify their offerings to include diverse dietary options, such as vegan, gluten-free, or paleo meals, stand to gain a competitive edge. This responsiveness not only attracts a broader customer base but also fosters brand loyalty. Entrepreneurs who prioritize adaptability in their service offerings will likely see increased customer satisfaction and retention, essential components in the health and wellness industry.

The rise of online personal training platforms exemplifies the necessity for adaptability in response to technological innovations. As virtual fitness solutions gained traction during the pandemic, franchises that were quick to enhance their digital presence and integrate user-friendly platforms thrived. This transition not only catered to existing clients but also attracted new users who preferred the convenience of online training. By continuously assessing and adapting to technological advancements, entrepreneurs can ensure their franchises remain relevant and appealing in a rapidly changing market.

Moreover, the growing emphasis on mental health and wellness coaching underscores the need for adaptability in service delivery. As awareness of mental health issues increases, franchises must be prepared to incorporate holistic approaches into their offerings. This could involve training staff in mental health first aid, integrating mindfulness practices into fitness routines, or offering workshops on stress management. By adapting to the shifting focus towards mental wellness, franchises can better serve their clients' comprehensive health needs, ultimately strengthening their market position.

Finally, the trend towards eco-friendly fitness products is another area where adaptability is vital. As consumers become more environmentally conscious, franchises that proactively incorporate sustainable practices and products into their business models can differentiate themselves from competitors. This adaptability not only meets consumer demand but also enhances brand reputation. Entrepreneurs who recognize and respond to these market shifts can create a sustainable franchise that resonates with a growing demographic of eco-minded consumers, ensuring ongoing relevance in the health and wellness sector.

03

Chapter 3: Mobile Fitness Studios

Concept and Benefits of Mobile Fitness

Mobile fitness is an innovative approach that leverages technology to deliver health and fitness services directly to users, enhancing convenience and accessibility. This concept encompasses a range of services, including mobile fitness studios, virtual personal training, and nutritional meal prep delivered to clients' doorsteps. By breaking down traditional barriers associated with gym memberships, such as location and schedule constraints, mobile fitness caters to the needs of a diverse clientele. Entrepreneurs venturing into this space can capitalize on the growing demand for flexible fitness solutions that fit seamlessly into busy lifestyles.

The benefits of mobile fitness extend beyond mere convenience. For franchise owners, this model offers a scalable business opportunity with lower overhead costs compared to traditional brick-and-mortar establishments. By utilizing mobile units or online platforms, entrepreneurs can reach a broader audience without the financial burden of maintaining a physical location. This flexibility allows for quicker expansion into new markets, providing the potential for higher returns on investment.

Additionally, mobile fitness can adapt to various niches within the health and wellness industry, such as corporate wellness programs or specialized classes like yoga for seniors, making it an attractive option for franchise lovers.

Mobile fitness also promotes a stronger sense of community and personalization in health and wellness. By offering tailored services directly to clients, businesses can foster closer relationships and create a supportive environment that encourages accountability and motivation. This personalized approach can result in higher client retention rates and referrals, essential components for any successful franchise. Furthermore, the ability to track progress through fitness technology and wearable devices enhances the client experience, allowing for real-time adjustments to training programs based on individual needs and preferences.

From a consumer perspective, the advantages of mobile fitness are significant. Clients benefit from the flexibility to engage in workouts or wellness activities at their convenience, which can lead to increased participation and a more consistent fitness regimen. The integration of nutritional meal prep services and health-focused meal delivery franchises further enhances this model, as clients can receive comprehensive support in their health journey without the added stress of meal planning. This holistic approach not only improves physical health but also contributes to mental well-being, creating a more balanced lifestyle.

In conclusion, the concept of mobile fitness presents a myriad of opportunities for entrepreneurs in the wellness industry. By embracing this model, franchise owners can cater to an evolving market that values convenience and personalization. As the demand for flexible health solutions continues to rise, investing in mobile fitness services not only aligns with contemporary consumer needs but also positions businesses for sustainable growth and success in the competitive health and wellness landscape.

Success Stories of Mobile Fitness Franchises

The rise of mobile fitness franchises illustrates a transformative shift in how health and wellness services are delivered. Entrepreneurs venturing into this domain have successfully harnessed the power of convenience and accessibility, catering to clients who seek personalized fitness solutions without the constraints of traditional gym settings. By offering on-demand services, these franchises have tapped into the growing demand for flexible fitness options, appealing to busy professionals, parents, and individuals with varying schedules.

One notable success story is that of a mobile personal training franchise that began with a single van and a handful of trainers. By focusing on providing tailored fitness experiences in clients' homes or local parks, the franchise rapidly expanded. Their unique approach not only attracted a diverse clientele but also fostered a sense of community among clients, who appreciated the social aspect of group workouts held outdoors. This innovative model allowed the franchise to scale quickly, establishing a presence in multiple cities and enhancing its brand recognition through word-of-mouth referrals and social media engagement.

Another exemplary case is that of a mobile nutritional meal prep service. This franchise recognized the need for healthy, convenient meal options in a market flooded with fast food. By partnering with local farms and nutritionists, they created a range of meal plans that cater to various dietary preferences and restrictions. Their focus on sustainability and fresh ingredients resonated with health-conscious consumers, leading to rapid growth. The franchise's ability to deliver freshly prepared meals directly to clients' doorsteps transformed not just the dining experience but also the health habits of its customers, illustrating the potential impact of mobile wellness solutions.

In the realm of wellness retreats, a franchise offering mobile wellness services has gained traction by providing on-site retreats at clients' homes or local venues. This franchise combines elements of fitness, mindfulness, and nutrition to create holistic wellness experiences tailored to individual or corporate needs. Their success can be attributed to a growing recognition of the importance of mental health and work-life balance, particularly in corporate environments. As businesses increasingly invest in employee wellbeing, this franchise has positioned itself as a leader in the market, offering customizable packages that enhance productivity and overall wellness.

Lastly, the emergence of mobile fitness technology and wearable devices has further fueled the success of fitness franchises. By integrating technology into their offerings, franchises have been able to provide real-time data and feedback to clients, enhancing the overall training experience. This tech-savvy approach has attracted a younger demographic eager for innovation in their fitness journeys. Through partnerships with tech developers, mobile fitness franchises are not only improving client engagement but also setting new trends in the industry, proving that adaptability and forward-thinking are key components in the pursuit of success in the health and wellness sector.

Key Considerations for Launching a Mobile Studio

Launching a mobile studio in the health and wellness sector requires careful planning and consideration of various factors that can influence success. One of the primary considerations is identifying the target market and understanding their specific needs. Entrepreneurs must conduct thorough market research to determine demographics, preferences, and trends within the local community. This information will guide decisions regarding the types of services offered, pricing structures, and marketing strategies. By aligning the mobile studio's offerings with the desires of potential clients, operators can enhance customer satisfaction and foster long-term loyalty.

Another essential aspect to consider is the legal and regulatory requirements that govern mobile fitness operations. Entrepreneurs should familiarize themselves with local zoning laws, health and safety regulations, and any necessary permits or licenses. This might include compliance with public health guidelines, especially regarding sanitation and hygiene practices. Additionally, it is vital to ensure that all staff members are properly certified and trained in their respective fields, whether that be fitness instruction, nutritional advice, or mental health coaching. Adhering to legal standards not only protects the business but also builds credibility with clients.

The logistics of operating a mobile studio also play a crucial role in launching a successful venture. This includes considerations such as vehicle selection, equipment storage, and transportation routes. Entrepreneurs must evaluate whether to purchase or lease a vehicle that meets the specific needs of their services, including adequate space for fitness equipment or meal prep supplies. Additionally, planning effective routes and schedules is necessary to optimize service delivery and minimize operational costs. Efficient logistics can significantly enhance the overall client experience, making it easier for customers to access services when and where they need them.

Marketing strategies tailored to the mobile format are another key consideration. Entrepreneurs should leverage digital platforms to reach a broader audience, using social media, email marketing, and online advertising to promote their unique offerings. Collaborations with local businesses, such as gyms, wellness retreats, or corporate offices, can also enhance visibility and attract new clients. Engaging storytelling that emphasizes the convenience and personalized approach of a mobile studio can help differentiate the business from traditional brick-and-mortar establishments. Building a strong brand presence online will be critical in attracting and retaining clientele.

Finally, financial planning is a fundamental aspect of launching a mobile studio. Entrepreneurs must develop a comprehensive budget that encompasses startup costs, ongoing operational expenses, and projected revenue streams. Considerations should include vehicle costs, equipment purchases, insurance, marketing expenses, and salaries for any staff. Establishing a clear financial plan helps ensure sustainability and growth while allowing for adjustments based on real-time performance metrics. By closely monitoring finances and adapting to market demands, mobile studio operators can position themselves for long-term success in the dynamic health and wellness industry.

04

Chapter 4: Nutritional Meal Prep Services

The Growing Demand for Meal Prep Services

The growing demand for meal prep services is becoming increasingly significant in today's fast-paced lifestyle. As more individuals recognize the importance of nutrition in achieving their health and fitness goals, the convenience and practicality of meal prep services have gained traction. Busy professionals, families, and health-conscious consumers are seeking efficient ways to maintain a balanced diet without sacrificing time or quality. This trend presents a unique opportunity for entrepreneurs and franchisees to capitalize on the rising interest in wellness and nutrition by offering tailored meal prep solutions. The health and fitness industry has seen a shift in consumer behavior, with an emphasis on personalized nutrition. Meal prep services align perfectly with this trend by providing customized meal plans that cater to specific dietary needs, preferences, and fitness goals. Whether it's high-protein meals for athletes or low-carb options for those seeking weight loss, the ability to offer personalized services can significantly enhance customer satisfaction and loyalty. Entrepreneurs who tap into this niche can establish themselves as leaders in the wellness sector, addressing the unique needs of their clientele.

In addition to personalization, the convenience factor plays a crucial role in the growing demand for meal prep services. As individuals juggle work commitments, family responsibilities, and personal fitness goals, the need for convenient meal options becomes paramount. Meal prep services eliminate the need for time-consuming grocery shopping and cooking, allowing consumers to focus on their health without the associated stress. Entrepreneurs in this space can leverage technology to streamline operations, offering online ordering and delivery systems that enhance the overall customer experience.

The environmental aspect of meal prep services is also gaining attention, as consumers become more conscious of their ecological footprint. Eco-friendly practices in sourcing ingredients, packaging, and delivery can attract a customer base that prioritizes sustainability. Entrepreneurs can differentiate their meal prep services by emphasizing local, organic produce and environmentally friendly packaging options. This approach not only caters to the growing eco-conscious consumer segment but also aligns with broader wellness trends that advocate for holistic health.

Finally, the integration of meal prep services with fitness and wellness programs creates an opportunity for synergistic growth. Partnerships with fitness studios, gyms, and wellness retreats can enhance the value proposition for both the meal prep service and the fitness provider. For instance, offering meal plans that complement specific workout regimens or wellness retreats can create a comprehensive approach to health for consumers. By positioning meal prep services as an integral part of the overall wellness journey, entrepreneurs can tap into a lucrative market that is poised for continued growth in the coming years.

Building a Brand in Nutritional Meal Prep

Building a brand in the nutritional meal prep industry requires a strategic approach that resonates with the values and needs of health-conscious consumers. Entrepreneurs seeking to establish a strong brand must first understand the unique selling proposition of their products. This involves not only offering healthy and delicious meal options but also emphasizing the convenience and time-saving aspects of meal prep services. As consumers become increasingly busy, a brand that positions itself as a solution to their meal planning challenges can stand out in a crowded marketplace.

A successful brand in nutritional meal prep should also prioritize transparency and quality in its offerings. This includes sourcing fresh, organic ingredients and providing clear nutritional information. By educating consumers about the benefits of each meal component, brands can foster trust and loyalty. Furthermore, engaging storytelling about the origins of the ingredients and the preparation process can create an emotional connection with customers, enhancing brand identity. This transparency is particularly crucial in the wellness industry, where consumers are more discerning about what they consume.

Incorporating eco-friendly practices can significantly enhance a brand's appeal in the nutritional meal prep niche. With growing awareness about sustainability, brands that adopt environmentally friendly packaging, prioritize local sourcing, and implement waste-reduction strategies can attract a dedicated customer base. This not only aligns with the values of many health-conscious consumers but also positions the brand as a leader in social responsibility. By communicating these initiatives through marketing channels, brands can differentiate themselves and build a community of like-minded individuals who support sustainable practices.

Effective marketing strategies are essential for building a recognizable brand in nutritional meal prep. Utilizing social media platforms to showcase meal options, customer testimonials, and behind-the-scenes content can create buzz and foster engagement. Collaborations with fitness influencers and wellness coaches can also broaden reach and enhance credibility. Additionally, offering promotions, referral programs, and loyalty rewards can incentivize customers to spread the word about the brand, facilitating organic growth. A strong online presence, coupled with an intuitive ordering system, can streamline the customer experience and reinforce brand loyalty.

Finally, continuous innovation is key to maintaining relevance and appeal in the nutritional meal prep market. Brands should stay attuned to emerging trends in health and wellness, such as plant-based diets or meal customization options. Regularly updating the menu to reflect seasonal ingredients or incorporating feedback from customers can keep offerings fresh and exciting. By fostering a culture of innovation and responsiveness, brands can not only retain existing customers but also attract new ones, ensuring long-term success in the competitive landscape of nutritional meal prep services.

Operational Challenges and Solutions

Operational challenges in the health and wellness franchise sector can significantly impact business growth and sustainability. Entrepreneurs must navigate various obstacles, including managing supply chains, ensuring consistent service delivery, and maintaining compliance with health regulations. For instance, mobile fitness studios often face logistical hurdles related to scheduling and equipment transport, which can lead to inefficiencies. Similarly, nutritional meal prep services encounter issues with sourcing fresh ingredients while keeping costs manageable. Addressing these challenges requires a strategic approach that combines effective management practices with innovative solutions tailored to the unique needs of each franchise niche.

One effective solution for mobile fitness studios is the implementation of advanced scheduling software that optimizes routes and time slots, ensuring maximum client engagement while minimizing downtime. Additionally, utilizing mobile apps can enhance customer interaction, allowing clients to easily book sessions and provide feedback. For nutritional meal prep services, developing strong relationships with local suppliers can lead to more reliable sourcing of quality ingredients. By establishing a network of trusted vendors, franchises can mitigate supply chain disruptions and enhance their ability to deliver fresh, healthy meals consistently.

Franchise owners in the wellness retreat and getaway market face the challenge of creating a unique experience that stands out in a competitive landscape. To address this, businesses can leverage partnerships with local wellness experts and holistic practitioners, integrating diverse wellness offerings such as yoga, meditation, and nutrition workshops. This collaboration not only enriches the guest experience but also fosters a community atmosphere that encourages repeat business and positive word-of-mouth referrals. Furthermore, incorporating eco-friendly practices into the retreat's operations can attract environmentally conscious consumers, enhancing the brand's appeal.

Online personal training platforms encounter the challenge of maintaining client engagement in a digital environment. To combat this issue, franchises can implement interactive features such as live-streamed classes, personalized fitness plans, and community forums. These elements promote accountability and foster a sense of belonging among clients. Additionally, utilizing fitness technology and wearable devices can provide real-time feedback to clients, enhancing their training experience and encouraging adherence to their fitness goals. This integration of technology not only improves client satisfaction but also positions the franchise as a leader in innovation within the wellness industry.

Finally, corporate wellness programs must address the challenge of convincing businesses of the value of investing in employee health. To effectively communicate benefits, franchise owners should gather data demonstrating the positive impact of wellness initiatives on employee productivity and morale. Creating customizable wellness packages that align with corporate goals can further entice businesses to invest. By offering solutions that cater to the specific needs of different organizations, franchises can establish themselves as essential partners in fostering a healthier workforce, ultimately driving growth in the health and wellness sector.

05

Chapter 5: Wellness Retreats and Getaway Franchises

Creating Unique Wellness Experiences

Creating unique wellness experiences is essential for entrepreneurs looking to make a mark in the health and wellness industry. As the market expands, consumers increasingly seek tailored solutions that resonate with their individual needs and preferences. By integrating personalization into wellness offerings, franchise owners can attract a broader clientele and foster deeper connections with their customers. This approach not only enhances customer satisfaction but also builds brand loyalty, creating a thriving business model in a competitive landscape.

One effective strategy for creating unique wellness experiences is to leverage technology. With the advent of fitness technology and wearable devices, businesses can provide personalized insights into clients' health and fitness journeys. For instance, franchises can offer mobile fitness studios equipped with apps that track user progress and deliver customized workout plans. These services not only cater to tech-savvy consumers but also provide an interactive experience that keeps clients engaged and motivated. By utilizing data analytics, franchises can further refine their offerings, ensuring they meet the evolving demands of their target audience.

Incorporating wellness retreats and getaway franchises into a business model can also set a brand apart. These experiential offerings create immersive environments where clients can escape the stresses of daily life while focusing on their health and well-being. By curating unique experiences—such as guided meditation sessions, nature hikes, and workshops on nutrition and mindfulness—entrepreneurs can cultivate a sense of community among participants. This not only enhances the overall experience but also encourages word-of-mouth marketing, as satisfied guests share their transformative journeys with others.

Another avenue for differentiation lies in specialized fitness classes tailored to specific demographics, such as seniors or individuals with unique health concerns. By addressing the distinct needs of these groups through targeted programming, franchises can tap into underserved markets. Offering classes like yoga for seniors or adaptive fitness sessions for those with mobility challenges not only fulfills a social responsibility but also opens new revenue streams. This focus on inclusivity not only benefits clients but positions the franchise as a leader in compassionate, client-centered wellness solutions.

Finally, prioritizing sustainability can create a unique selling proposition in the wellness space. Entrepreneurs can develop eco-friendly fitness products and nutritional meal prep services that align with consumers' growing concerns about environmental impact. By promoting green practices—such as using biodegradable packaging for meal deliveries or sourcing equipment from sustainable materials—franchises can attract environmentally conscious customers. This commitment to sustainability not only enhances brand reputation but also resonates with a market increasingly focused on holistic health, which encompasses both individual well-being and environmental stewardship.

Target Markets for Wellness Retreats

The wellness retreat industry has seen remarkable growth in recent years, attracting a diverse clientele seeking relaxation, rejuvenation, and holistic health solutions. Entrepreneurs in this space must identify and understand their target markets to build successful wellness retreat franchises. The primary audience consists of health-conscious individuals looking to escape the stresses of daily life, particularly those aged 25 to 55. This demographic often prioritizes wellness and self-care, making them prime candidates for immersive experiences that promote mental and physical well-being.

In addition to individual clients, corporate wellness programs represent a significant market for wellness retreats. Companies are increasingly recognizing the value of investing in their employees' health. By offering retreats as part of corporate wellness initiatives, businesses can enhance employee morale, reduce burnout, and foster team cohesion. This segment presents a lucrative opportunity for retreat franchises to design tailored packages that focus on stress management, team-building activities, and overall health improvement, appealing to organizations eager to enhance productivity and employee satisfaction.

Another vital target market for wellness retreats includes niche groups focused on specific health needs or interests. For instance, retreats that cater to seniors with specialized fitness classes, such as gentle yoga or guided meditation, can attract an older demographic seeking low-impact wellness solutions. Similarly, retreats targeting mental health and wellness coaching can draw individuals facing stress, anxiety, or burnout. Entrepreneurs should consider developing programs that address the unique challenges and interests of these groups, ensuring a personalized approach that resonates with potential clients.

Young professionals and millennials also represent a key demographic for wellness retreats, as they increasingly prioritize experiences over material possessions. This group often seeks opportunities for personal growth, social connection, and mindfulness practices. Marketing strategies that highlight unique experiences, such as nature-based activities, digital detox options, and community-building exercises, can effectively engage this audience. Additionally, leveraging social media and influencer partnerships can enhance visibility and appeal to this tech-savvy market segment.

Lastly, the rise of eco-conscious consumers has created an opportunity for wellness retreats that emphasize sustainability and environmental responsibility. Entrepreneurs can attract clients who prioritize eco-friendly practices by incorporating green initiatives into their retreats, such as organic meal preparation, sustainable accommodations, and nature conservation activities. By aligning wellness with environmental stewardship, retreat franchises can tap into a growing market of individuals eager to support businesses that reflect their values, ultimately enhancing their appeal and fostering long-term loyalty.

Marketing Strategies for Retreat Franchises

Marketing strategies for retreat franchises in the health and wellness sector must be tailored to resonate with a diverse audience seeking holistic experiences. Firstly, establishing a strong brand identity is crucial. The brand should communicate the core values of wellness, sustainability, and community. Utilizing storytelling techniques can help convey the unique narrative of the retreat, whether focusing on transformative experiences, expert-led programs, or the serene natural environment. Visual branding elements, such as logos and color schemes that evoke tranquility and health, should be consistently applied across all marketing materials, from websites to social media platforms.

Digital marketing plays a pivotal role in promoting retreat franchises. A well-optimized website that showcases the retreat's offerings, testimonials, and expert instructors can significantly enhance visibility. Search engine optimization (SEO) strategies should be employed to ensure that potential customers can easily find the retreat when searching for wellness experiences online. Furthermore, social media platforms like Instagram and Facebook are essential for engaging potential clients. Sharing high-quality images, videos of retreat activities, and live Q&A sessions can foster a sense of community and attract individuals interested in holistic health.

Email marketing remains a powerful tool for nurturing leads and maintaining engagement with previous attendees. Creating a subscription-based newsletter can provide valuable content, such as wellness tips, nutrition advice, and exclusive offers for upcoming retreats. Segmenting the email list based on customer interests allows for more personalized communication, enhancing the likelihood of repeat business. Additionally, incorporating referral programs can incentivize past participants to share their positive experiences with friends and family, further expanding the retreat's reach.

Collaboration with influencers and wellness professionals can amplify marketing efforts significantly. Partnering with thought leaders in the health and wellness space can enhance credibility and expand the retreat's audience. Influencers can share their personal experiences at the retreat, providing authentic testimonials that resonate with their followers. Additionally, co-hosting workshops or events with reputable health coaches, chefs, or fitness experts can attract new clientele while enriching the retreat's offerings.

Finally, local and corporate partnerships can broaden the retreat's marketing scope. Collaborating with local businesses, such as gyms, yoga studios, and health food stores, can create mutually beneficial promotional opportunities. Offering corporate wellness programs can also tap into the growing trend of companies investing in employee well-being. By presenting customized retreat experiences designed to promote team bonding and stress relief, retreat franchises can attract business clients looking for unique employee wellness solutions. Through a combination of strategic branding, digital outreach, and community partnerships, retreat franchises can effectively position themselves in the competitive wellness market.

Chapter 6: Online Personal Training Platforms

The Shift to Digital Fitness Solutions

The rise of digital fitness solutions has transformed the landscape of the health and wellness industry, creating new opportunities for entrepreneurs and franchise owners. As technology continues to evolve, businesses are shifting from traditional brick-and-mortar models to more innovative and flexible digital platforms. This transition not only meets the growing consumer demand for convenience and accessibility but also allows fitness and wellness providers to reach a broader audience. Entrepreneurs must understand these trends to position their franchises effectively in an increasingly competitive market.

Mobile fitness studios and online personal training platforms have gained traction as consumers seek personalized solutions that fit their busy lifestyles. These digital offerings enable customers to engage with fitness professionals from the comfort of their homes or wherever they may be. As a result, franchise owners can create scalable business models that leverage technology for customer engagement and retention. By integrating virtual classes, one-on-one coaching, and on-demand workout sessions, franchises can differentiate themselves in a crowded marketplace and cater to a diverse clientele.

Nutritional meal prep services and health-focused meal delivery franchises are also embracing the digital shift. By utilizing mobile apps and online ordering systems, these businesses can streamline their operations and enhance the customer experience. The ability to customize meal plans and deliver nutritious options directly to consumers' doorsteps aligns with the growing trend towards health-conscious eating. Entrepreneurs in the wellness industry can capitalize on this by combining digital marketing strategies with user-friendly technology to attract and retain customers who prioritize convenience and quality in their nutrition choices.

Moreover, wellness retreats and getaway franchises are increasingly incorporating digital elements into their offerings. Virtual retreats, online workshops, and wellness coaching sessions provide opportunities for participants to engage with experts and learn about mental health and wellness from anywhere in the world. This hybrid model not only expands the reach of these businesses but also allows for greater flexibility, enabling participants to choose their preferred mode of engagement. Entrepreneurs can harness this trend to create unique experiences that blend in-person and virtual offerings, appealing to a wider audience.

The integration of fitness technology and wearable devices into the wellness landscape further illustrates the shift to digital fitness solutions. Entrepreneurs can explore partnerships with tech companies to develop innovative products that enhance the fitness experience. This includes tracking apps, fitness wearables, and eco-friendly fitness products designed to promote sustainable health practices. By staying ahead of these trends and embracing the digital transformation, business owners in the health and wellness sector can establish themselves as leaders in a rapidly changing industry, ensuring long-term success and growth in their franchises.

Key Features of Successful Online Platforms

Successful online platforms in the health and wellness industry share several key features that contribute to their effectiveness and appeal. First and foremost, user experience is paramount. A seamless, intuitive interface allows users to easily navigate the platform, whether they are searching for meal prep services, booking a wellness retreat, or signing up for online personal training. Well-designed platforms prioritize accessibility and responsiveness, ensuring that users can effortlessly engage with content and services across various devices. This commitment to user experience fosters higher engagement rates and customer satisfaction, essential for retaining clients in a competitive market.

Another critical feature is the integration of community-building elements. Online platforms that successfully foster a sense of community encourage user interaction through forums, social media groups, and live events. This sense of belonging not only enhances user experience but also drives loyalty. For entrepreneurs in the wellness sector, creating a vibrant community can differentiate their platform from competitors. Features such as user-generated content, testimonials, and interactive challenges can cultivate a supportive environment where clients feel motivated and connected to others on similar wellness journeys.

Data analytics capabilities are increasingly vital for online platforms in health and wellness. By harnessing user data, entrepreneurs can gain insights into customer preferences, behavior patterns, and engagement levels. This information enables informed decision-making regarding product offerings, marketing strategies, and service improvements. Platforms that utilize data analytics can tailor their services to meet the evolving needs of their clientele, ultimately enhancing the effectiveness of wellness programs and increasing customer retention.

Another essential feature is the provision of personalized services. Successful online platforms utilize technology to offer tailored solutions to users, whether through customized workout plans, personalized meal prep options, or targeted mental health coaching. By leveraging artificial intelligence and machine learning, platforms can analyze individual user data and preferences to deliver bespoke recommendations. This level of personalization not only increases user satisfaction but also helps clients achieve their health and wellness goals more effectively, further solidifying their commitment to the platform.

Lastly, a successful online platform must prioritize security and privacy. Users need to trust that their personal and financial information is safe while engaging with the platform. Implementing robust security measures, including encryption and secure payment gateways, is crucial in building this trust. Transparent privacy policies that outline how user data is collected, used, and protected can enhance credibility and reassure clients. By prioritizing security, entrepreneurs can create a safe environment that encourages users to engage more deeply with their health and wellness journey, ultimately driving the platform's success.

Monetization Strategies for Online Training

Monetization strategies for online training encompass a variety of approaches tailored to the unique needs of the health and wellness industry. Entrepreneurs can leverage subscription-based models, where clients pay a recurring fee for access to a library of training videos, live classes, and personalized coaching sessions. This model not only ensures a steady stream of income but also fosters a sense of community as members engage with each other and the trainers. Additionally, offering tiered subscription levels can cater to different budgets and preferences, enhancing customer retention and satisfaction.

Another effective monetization strategy is the implementation of pay-per-class or pay-per-session options. This approach allows clients to purchase individual classes or sessions without a long-term commitment, making fitness more accessible to a broader audience. It is particularly appealing for those hesitant to commit to a full subscription or those looking to try out specific programs, such as specialized fitness classes like yoga for seniors. By providing flexible pricing options, entrepreneurs can attract a diverse clientele while maximizing revenue opportunities.

Affiliate marketing is also a powerful tool for monetizing online training platforms. By partnering with eco-friendly fitness products, nutritional meal prep services, and fitness technology brands, entrepreneurs can earn commissions on sales generated through their platforms. This not only diversifies income streams but also enhances the training experience for clients by recommending complementary products that align with their wellness goals. Incorporating affiliate links into training materials and promotional content can create a seamless shopping experience for customers while boosting profitability.

Incorporating corporate wellness programs into the online training model presents another lucrative avenue for monetization. Businesses are increasingly recognizing the value of investing in the health and well-being of their employees, leading to a rising demand for tailored fitness programs and workshops. By offering customized packages for companies, online training platforms can attract large groups of clients, resulting in significant revenue growth. This strategy not only benefits the entrepreneurs financially but also promotes a healthier workforce, creating a win-win scenario.

Lastly, wellness retreats and getaway franchises can be integrated into online training offerings, providing an exceptional value proposition. Entrepreneurs can market exclusive access to virtual retreats or workshops, allowing clients to experience immersive training sessions from the comfort of their homes. This hybrid model can also promote in-person events, driving interest and participation in future retreats. By blending online training with experiential offerings, businesses can create a comprehensive wellness ecosystem that appeals to health-conscious consumers, driving both engagement and profitability.

Chapter 7: Eco-Friendly Fitness Products

The Importance of Sustainability in Fitness

Sustainability in fitness has emerged as a critical consideration for entrepreneurs and business leaders within the health and wellness sector. As consumers become increasingly aware of environmental issues, their preferences are shifting towards businesses that prioritize eco-friendly practices. This trend is particularly relevant in the fitness industry, where equipment, facilities, and services can have significant environmental impacts. By embracing sustainable practices, fitness franchises can not only attract a conscientious customer base but also contribute positively to the planet, creating a win-win scenario for both business and society.

One of the primary areas where sustainability can be integrated into fitness businesses is through the use of eco-friendly products and equipment. Many companies are now producing fitness gear made from recycled materials or sustainable resources. Entrepreneurs can differentiate their offerings by sourcing equipment that minimizes environmental impact, such as biodegradable yoga mats or energy-efficient machines. This not only appeals to eco-conscious consumers but also enhances brand reputation, as businesses that demonstrate social responsibility are often viewed more favorably in the marketplace.

In addition to product offerings, sustainability can be woven into the operational practices of fitness franchises. This includes adopting energy-efficient technologies, implementing recycling programs, and reducing waste in facilities. For instance, mobile fitness studios can utilize electric vehicles or bicycles for transportation, while nutritional meal prep services can focus on sourcing local and organic ingredients to minimize their carbon footprint. By prioritizing sustainable operations, franchise owners can reduce costs in the long term while also enhancing their appeal to environmentally aware clients.

The mental health aspect of wellness is also significantly bolstered by a commitment to sustainability. Research shows that engaging with nature can lead to improved mental well-being. Wellness retreats and getaway franchises can capitalize on this by offering programs that incorporate outdoor activities and natural settings. By promoting a connection to the environment, these businesses not only support the mental health of their clients but also highlight the importance of preserving the very spaces that facilitate such healing experiences.

Finally, sustainability in fitness is not just about immediate benefits; it creates opportunities for innovation and growth within the industry. As consumers demand more sustainable options, businesses that adapt to these changes will find new niches to explore, such as eco-friendly fitness technology and solutions for corporate wellness programs that emphasize environmental stewardship. By aligning their business models with sustainable practices, entrepreneurs can position themselves at the forefront of a rapidly evolving market, ensuring long-term success and relevance in the health and wellness landscape.

Market Opportunities for Eco-Friendly Products

The rise of eco-conscious consumerism presents a significant market opportunity for entrepreneurs in the health and wellness sector. As awareness of environmental issues increases, consumers are actively seeking products and services that align with their values, particularly in the realms of fitness and wellness. This shift is evident in various niches, including mobile fitness studios, nutritional meal prep services, and wellness retreats. Entrepreneurs who can integrate eco-friendly practices into their business models not only cater to a growing demographic but also position themselves as leaders in sustainability within the industry.

In the realm of fitness technology and wearable devices, opportunities abound for innovations that prioritize sustainability. Companies can focus on creating energy-efficient products, utilizing sustainable materials, and implementing recycling programs for old devices. Additionally, the development of apps that promote eco-friendly fitness routines or track carbon footprints related to workouts can attract environmentally conscious consumers. By emphasizing technology that supports both health and the planet, entrepreneurs can tap into a lucrative market while contributing positively to environmental stewardship.

Franchising offers a unique avenue for eco-friendly businesses to expand their reach. Franchise models that emphasize sustainable practices can attract partners who are passionate about health and the environment. For instance, health-focused meal delivery franchises can incorporate locally sourced, organic ingredients to minimize their carbon footprint. Similarly, wellness retreats can design eco-friendly accommodations and activities that promote both physical and mental health. By creating a franchise network centered on sustainability, business owners can leverage shared values and practices to foster community and loyalty among franchisees and customers alike.

Online personal training platforms also have significant potential for incorporating eco-friendly elements. Trainers can promote virtual workouts that reduce transportation emissions and encourage clients to engage in outdoor activities that connect them with nature. Additionally, offering courses on sustainable living, nutrition, and wellness can appeal to an audience eager to adopt eco-friendly lifestyles. Entrepreneurs in this space can develop a brand that stands for both fitness and environmental responsibility, attracting consumers who are looking to make healthier choices for themselves and the planet.

Lastly, as corporate wellness programs gain traction, there is an opportunity for businesses to integrate eco-friendly practices into their offerings. Companies can implement initiatives such as outdoor team-building exercises, green office environments, and nutrition workshops focused on sustainable eating. By promoting wellness in a way that also considers environmental impact, entrepreneurs can help organizations foster healthier workplaces while also appealing to a workforce that increasingly values sustainability. The intersection of eco-friendliness and wellness presents a dynamic opportunity for growth and innovation in the health and wellness industry.

Building a Green Brand in Fitness

Building a green brand in the fitness industry is increasingly essential as consumers become more environmentally conscious. Entrepreneurs and franchise owners must recognize that sustainability can greatly enhance brand loyalty and market reach. By adopting eco-friendly practices and promoting a green ethos, fitness brands can differentiate themselves in a crowded marketplace. This approach not only attracts a niche audience but also aligns with the values of many modern consumers who prioritize sustainability when making purchasing decisions.

One effective strategy for building a green brand is to incorporate sustainable practices into everyday operations. For instance, mobile fitness studios can utilize eco-friendly vehicles and equipment made from recycled materials. Nutritional meal prep services can source local, organic ingredients to minimize their carbon footprint while supporting local farmers. Franchises focused on wellness retreats can implement green building practices at their facilities, such as using energy-efficient appliances and sustainable materials. By showcasing these efforts, businesses can enhance their credibility and appeal to environmentally conscious customers.

Marketing plays a crucial role in establishing a green brand identity. Fitness businesses should highlight their sustainability initiatives through various channels, including social media, websites, and promotional materials. Collaborations with eco-friendly fitness product suppliers or partnerships with environmental organizations can further strengthen a brand's commitment to sustainability. Online personal training platforms can promote their green practices by emphasizing virtual sessions that reduce travel emissions. Creating informative content that educates consumers about the importance of eco-friendly choices in fitness can also resonate with a wider audience.

Investing in eco-friendly fitness technology and wearable devices can also help solidify a brand's green reputation. Businesses can offer products that not only enhance fitness experiences but also promote sustainability, such as devices that track energy expenditure and encourage users to engage in eco-friendly activities. Specialized fitness classes, such as yoga for seniors, can incorporate natural elements into their sessions, such as outdoor settings or the use of sustainable materials for props. By integrating sustainability into the core of their offerings, fitness brands can create a lasting impact on their customers and the environment.

Ultimately, building a green brand in the fitness industry requires a commitment to ongoing improvement and innovation. Entrepreneurs must continuously seek new ways to enhance their sustainability practices and engage with their communities. Corporate wellness programs can incorporate eco-friendly initiatives that promote employee health while fostering a culture of environmental responsibility. As the demand for sustainable solutions continues to grow, fitness businesses that prioritize green branding will not only thrive but also contribute to a healthier planet and society.

08

Chapter 8: Mental Health and Wellness Coaching

Understanding the Connection Between Fitness and Mental Health

Understanding the connection between fitness and mental health is essential for anyone involved in the wellness industry, particularly entrepreneurs and franchise owners. Numerous studies have established that physical activity plays a crucial role in enhancing mental well-being. Engaging in regular exercise can lead to the release of endorphins, often referred to as "feel-good" hormones, which can alleviate symptoms of anxiety and depression. This biological response underscores the importance of integrating fitness programs into mental health strategies, highlighting the potential for wellness franchises to address both physical and psychological needs.

For franchise owners in the health and wellness sector, understanding this connection can inform the development of more comprehensive services. By offering programs that blend fitness with mental health support, businesses can attract a broader clientele seeking holistic wellness solutions. For example, mobile fitness studios can incorporate mindfulness practices such as yoga or meditation into their offerings, creating an environment that fosters mental clarity alongside physical strength. This dual approach not only enhances customer satisfaction but also positions franchises as leaders in the holistic wellness movement.

Moreover, the corporate wellness trend has amplified the demand for integrated fitness and mental health solutions. Companies are increasingly recognizing the impact of employee well-being on productivity and workplace morale. By implementing corporate wellness programs that include fitness classes, mental health workshops, and nutritional guidance, franchise owners can create tailored solutions that benefit both employees and employers. This approach not only improves mental health outcomes but also fosters a culture of wellness that can significantly reduce healthcare costs in the long run.

Online personal training platforms and wellness retreats also play pivotal roles in bridging fitness with mental health. The flexibility of online training allows clients to access tailored workout plans and mental wellness resources from the comfort of their homes. Meanwhile, wellness retreats provide immersive experiences that focus on rejuvenation and mental clarity through fitness, nutrition, and mindfulness practices. These models present franchise opportunities that cater to the growing consumer demand for comprehensive health solutions, emphasizing the importance of mental health in overall wellness.

Lastly, the rise of fitness technology and wearable devices offers exciting prospects for enhancing both physical fitness and mental well-being. By leveraging data from fitness trackers, franchise owners can provide personalized insights that help clients set and achieve their health goals. Additionally, apps and platforms that promote mental health through guided workouts or stress-reduction techniques can create a more engaging user experience. This integration not only drives customer loyalty but also reinforces the understanding that mental and physical fitness are intricately connected, paving the way for innovative services in the wellness franchise landscape.

Developing a Coaching Program

Developing a coaching program is a pivotal aspect of establishing a successful franchise in the health and wellness industry. This program should not only align with the overarching goals of the franchise but also cater to the specific needs of your target audience. Entrepreneurs must first determine the focus of their coaching program. This could range from physical fitness training and nutritional guidance to mental health support and wellness retreats. By identifying a niche, businesses can tailor their offerings, ensuring that they meet the unique demands of their clientele, whether they are individuals seeking personal growth or companies looking to enhance employee wellness.

Once the focus is established, the next step is to design the curriculum of the coaching program. This involves outlining the key topics, methods, and outcomes that will be addressed during the coaching sessions. For instance, a program directed at online personal training might include modules on exercise science, client engagement techniques, and digital fitness technologies. Conversely, a coaching program aimed at corporate wellness could incorporate stress management techniques, team-building exercises, and health assessments. The curriculum should be both comprehensive and adaptable, allowing for customization based on the specific needs of clients and the evolving landscape of health and wellness.

Recruiting qualified coaches is crucial for the success of the program. Coaches should not only possess the necessary certifications and expertise but also embody the core values of the franchise. They must be passionate about health and wellness and adept at building rapport with clients. When selecting coaches, consider their experience in specialized areas such as yoga for seniors or nutritional meal prep services. A diverse team can enhance the richness of the program, offering varied perspectives and approaches that cater to a broader range of clients. Continued professional development opportunities for coaches will ensure they stay updated with the latest trends and research in the health and wellness field.

Marketing the coaching program effectively is essential for attracting clients and building a loyal customer base. Utilize multiple channels, including social media, email marketing, and partnerships with local businesses, to promote the program. Highlight success stories and testimonials from past participants to build credibility and demonstrate the value of the coaching services. Creating engaging content, such as informative blog posts or videos that provide insights into the coaching process, can also help to generate interest and establish authority in the wellness sector. Additionally, consider offering introductory workshops or free consultations to give potential clients a taste of what the program entails.

Finally, evaluating the effectiveness of the coaching program should be an ongoing process. Collect feedback from participants regularly to assess their satisfaction, progress, and areas for improvement. This can be achieved through surveys, one-on-one check-ins, or group discussions. Analyzing data on client outcomes will provide valuable insights into the program's impact and help identify any necessary adjustments. By fostering a culture of continuous improvement and responsiveness to client needs, franchise owners can enhance their coaching program, ensuring it remains relevant and effective in the ever-evolving health and wellness landscape.

Marketing Mental Health Services

Marketing mental health services requires a nuanced approach that respects the sensitivity of the subject while effectively reaching the target audience. Entrepreneurs and franchise owners in the health and wellness industry must recognize that mental health is an integral part of overall well-being. Therefore, marketing strategies should focus on creating awareness, destigmatizing mental health issues, and highlighting the benefits of available services. By employing a compassionate and informed messaging strategy, businesses can connect with potential clients who may be seeking support.

Digital marketing presents a powerful avenue for promoting mental health services. Social media platforms, blogs, and podcasts can be utilized to share valuable content that educates the audience about mental health topics, such as anxiety management, mindfulness practices, and the importance of seeking help. Engaging with the community through online forums and webinars can also create an environment of trust and openness. By positioning themselves as thought leaders in mental health, entrepreneurs can attract individuals who are eager to learn and participate in wellness programs.

Partnerships with local businesses and organizations can further enhance the visibility of mental health services. Collaborating with gyms, wellness retreats, or corporate wellness programs allows for cross-promotion, where clients seeking physical fitness may also become interested in mental health support. Offering workshops or seminars at these venues can introduce mental health services to a broader audience, demonstrating the interconnectedness of physical and mental well-being. Additionally, educational materials can be distributed in these spaces to provide information about available resources.

Promoting mental health services through targeted advertising can also prove effective. Utilizing demographic data and psychographics, businesses can create campaigns that resonate with specific audiences, whether they are seniors seeking specialized fitness classes or employees looking for corporate wellness solutions. Online advertisements, email marketing, and search engine optimization can be tailored to reach individuals actively searching for mental health resources. Highlighting success stories and testimonials can further build credibility and encourage potential clients to seek help.

Finally, creating a supportive community around mental health services can enhance customer loyalty and retention. By fostering an environment where clients feel safe to share their experiences, businesses can encourage ongoing engagement and referrals. Incorporating online support groups, feedback channels, and follow-up sessions can ensure that clients feel valued and understood. As mental health becomes an increasingly important aspect of overall wellness, entrepreneurs in the health and wellness industry must prioritize marketing strategies that are not only effective but also empathetic and supportive.

Chapter 9: Corporate Wellness Programs

The Rise of Corporate Wellness Initiatives

The rise of corporate wellness initiatives marks a significant shift in how organizations approach employee health and well-being. In recent years, companies have begun to recognize that investing in their employees' health not only improves morale but also enhances productivity and reduces healthcare costs. This trend has led to the development of comprehensive wellness programs that encompass physical fitness, mental health, nutritional guidance, and overall lifestyle improvements. As entrepreneurs and franchise operators explore opportunities within this burgeoning sector, understanding the elements that contribute to successful corporate wellness initiatives becomes crucial.

A key factor driving the popularity of corporate wellness programs is the growing awareness of the link between employee well-being and organizational performance. Studies have shown that healthier employees tend to be more engaged, less likely to take sick days, and more productive overall. This realization has prompted businesses to adopt wellness strategies that go beyond traditional health benefits. Many organizations are now offering fitness classes, mental health resources, and nutritional counseling as part of their employee benefits package. As a result, the demand for specialized services such as online personal training platforms and mobile fitness studios has surged, creating new avenues for franchise opportunities.

Incorporating wellness retreats and getaway franchises into corporate wellness strategies has also gained traction. These retreats provide employees with immersive experiences that focus on relaxation, mindfulness, and team bonding. Companies recognize that offering such experiences can lead to improved mental health and decreased burnout among staff. Entrepreneurs in the wellness industry can capitalize on this trend by creating retreat programs that cater to corporate clients, combining fitness activities with relaxation techniques and nutritional workshops. This holistic approach addresses the diverse needs of employees while fostering a culture of well-being within organizations.

Moreover, the integration of technology into corporate wellness initiatives is reshaping how companies engage their workforce in health-related activities. Fitness technology and wearable devices allow employees to track their physical activity, monitor their health metrics, and participate in challenges that encourage healthy competition. This data-driven approach empowers individuals to take charge of their health while providing employers with valuable insights into employee engagement levels. Entrepreneurs can explore franchise opportunities that focus on developing innovative wellness technologies or providing eco-friendly fitness products that align with corporate sustainability goals.

As the corporate landscape continues to evolve, mental health and wellness coaching have emerged as essential components of comprehensive wellness programs. Organizations are increasingly prioritizing mental health support to combat workplace stress and promote a healthy work-life balance. This growing emphasis creates a demand for specialized services, such as mental health coaching and tailored wellness workshops. Entrepreneurs who can provide these services in a franchise model will find themselves positioned at the forefront of a movement that prioritizes employee well-being as a key driver of organizational success. By embracing the rise of corporate wellness initiatives, businesses and entrepreneurs alike can contribute to a healthier, more productive workforce while fostering a culture of well-being in the workplace.

Designing Effective Programs for Businesses

Designing effective programs for businesses in the health and wellness sector requires a strategic approach that aligns with the unique needs of the target audience. Franchises must consider the diverse niches within this industry, such as mobile fitness studios, nutritional meal prep services, and corporate wellness programs. By understanding the specific demands of these segments, entrepreneurs can create tailored offerings that resonate with potential clients. This approach not only enhances customer satisfaction but also fosters brand loyalty, crucial for long-term success in a competitive market.

To develop impactful programs, businesses should prioritize research and data analysis. By gathering insights on current trends, consumer preferences, and the competitive landscape, entrepreneurs can identify gaps in the market. For instance, the rise of online personal training platforms and eco-friendly fitness products highlights a growing consumer demand for convenience and sustainability. Leveraging this data allows businesses to innovate and refine their services, ensuring they stay ahead of industry trends while addressing the evolving needs of their clients.

Collaboration with experts in various wellness fields is another essential element in program design. Engaging with nutritionists, fitness trainers, mental health professionals, and technology specialists can provide valuable perspectives and enhance the credibility of the programs offered. For example, incorporating mental health and wellness coaching into fitness classes can create a comprehensive approach that addresses both physical and mental well-being. Such collaborations not only improve program quality but also expand the network of referrals and partnerships, ultimately driving business growth.

An effective program must also be adaptable to cater to different demographics and preferences. Specialized fitness classes, such as yoga for seniors, demonstrate the importance of inclusivity and tailored offerings. By recognizing the varying needs of clients based on age, fitness level, and lifestyle, businesses can design programs that are both accessible and engaging. This adaptability can significantly increase participation rates and overall program effectiveness, making it essential for entrepreneurs to remain flexible and responsive to feedback.

Lastly, marketing plays a critical role in the success of health and wellness programs. By employing targeted marketing strategies that highlight the unique benefits of their offerings, businesses can effectively reach their desired audience. Utilizing social media, email campaigns, and community events can create awareness and generate interest in new programs. Moreover, showcasing success stories and testimonials can enhance credibility, encouraging potential clients to engage with the brand. A well-executed marketing plan not only drives enrollment but also positions the franchise as a leader in the health and wellness industry.

Measuring Success and Impact

Measuring success and impact in the health and wellness franchise sector requires a multifaceted approach that encompasses both quantitative and qualitative metrics. For entrepreneurs and business leaders, defining success should begin with establishing clear, measurable objectives aligned with their overall mission. Key performance indicators (KPIs) such as customer retention rates, revenue growth, and client satisfaction scores provide a numerical basis for evaluating performance. Additionally, franchise owners should consider metrics tailored to their specific niche, such as the number of clients participating in specialized fitness classes or the frequency of meal deliveries in nutritional meal prep services. Incorporating client feedback is essential for gauging the impact of services offered. Regular surveys and focus groups can provide valuable insights into customer experiences and satisfaction levels. For instance, a mobile fitness studio may assess the effectiveness of its programs by soliciting testimonials from participants about their progress and overall enjoyment. This qualitative data can be as crucial as financial metrics, revealing areas for improvement and opportunities for innovation. By actively listening to clients, franchise owners position themselves to adapt their offerings to better meet the needs of their target market.

Moreover, the impact of health and wellness franchises extends beyond individual client success to encompass community wellness. Measuring this broader impact can involve tracking community engagement initiatives, partnerships with local health organizations, and participation in wellness events. Entrepreneurs in the sector should consider how their efforts contribute to the overall health of the communities they serve. For instance, a franchise specializing in corporate wellness programs can evaluate its success by assessing employee health metrics and workplace satisfaction levels, demonstrating the tangible benefits of their services beyond the immediate client relationship.

In the age of technology, utilizing data analytics can significantly enhance the ability to measure success. Fitness technology and wearable devices provide real-time data that can be leveraged to assess client adherence and progress. Franchise owners can analyze usage patterns, engagement levels, and health outcomes to refine their offerings effectively. Similarly, online personal training platforms can track client progress through app-based metrics, allowing for personalized adjustments that enhance the effectiveness of their programs. By embracing technology, franchises can create a more responsive and data-driven approach to measuring their impact.

Finally, establishing a culture of continuous improvement is vital for long-term success in the health and wellness industry. This involves regularly reviewing performance metrics, client feedback, and industry trends to identify areas for growth. By fostering a mindset that embraces change and innovation, entrepreneurs and franchise owners can ensure they remain competitive and relevant in a rapidly evolving market. Whether it's through developing new eco-friendly fitness products or expanding into wellness retreats, the ability to measure success and impact accurately will empower franchises to make strategic decisions that enhance their offerings and contribute positively to the health landscape.

Chapter 10: Specialized Fitness Classes

Identifying Niche Markets (e.g., Yoga for Seniors)

Identifying niche markets is crucial for entrepreneurs seeking to thrive in the competitive landscape of health and wellness. A niche market allows businesses to cater to a specific segment of consumers with tailored products and services. For instance, yoga for seniors is an exemplary niche that addresses the unique needs of an aging population. This demographic often seeks low-impact exercise options that enhance flexibility, balance, and overall well-being. By focusing on this niche, entrepreneurs can create targeted marketing strategies and develop programs that resonate with older adults, ultimately fostering a loyal customer base.

To successfully tap into niche markets, it's essential to conduct thorough market research. Understanding the demographic characteristics, interests, and pain points of your target audience will inform your business model and offerings. In the case of yoga for seniors, research may reveal that many older adults are concerned about injury, chronic pain, or the complexity of traditional yoga classes. By addressing these concerns through gentle, accessible classes and supportive environments, businesses can position themselves as leaders in this specialized field.

Furthermore, leveraging partnerships can enhance visibility and credibility within niche markets. Collaborating with local senior centers, retirement communities, or healthcare providers can create referral networks that drive customer engagement. For example, a franchise offering senior yoga classes could partner with physical therapists who recommend their programs as part of a comprehensive rehabilitation plan. By establishing these relationships, entrepreneurs can effectively reach their target audience and build trust within the community.

Marketing strategies should also reflect the unique attributes of the niche. For yoga for seniors, the messaging should emphasize health benefits such as improved mobility, reduced stress, and social connections. Utilizing platforms like social media, community newsletters, and local events can help create awareness and attract potential clients. Additionally, showcasing testimonials from participants can provide social proof, illustrating how the program has positively impacted the lives of seniors.

Finally, entrepreneurs should remain adaptable to the evolving needs and preferences of their niche market. Trends in health and wellness are constantly shifting, and staying informed about these changes is vital. For instance, the growing emphasis on mental health may lead to a demand for integrative approaches that combine yoga with mindfulness practices. By continuously assessing market dynamics and being willing to innovate, businesses can ensure long-term success and sustainability within their niche markets.

Creating Inclusive Fitness Programs

Creating inclusive fitness programs is essential for ensuring that health and wellness services are accessible to everyone, regardless of their background, abilities, or fitness levels. With the growing diversity in the population, entrepreneurs in the health and wellness sectors must design programs that cater to a wide range of individuals. This requires a commitment to understanding the unique needs of various demographics, including seniors, individuals with disabilities, and those from different cultural backgrounds. By fostering an inclusive environment, fitness businesses not only broaden their customer base but also enhance the overall community wellness.

One effective approach to developing inclusive fitness programs is to incorporate adaptive equipment and training methods. This can involve offering specialized classes that accommodate individuals with physical limitations, such as chair yoga or low-impact aerobics. For mobile fitness studios, ensuring that vehicles are equipped to transport adaptive equipment can make a significant difference. Additionally, investing in training for staff members on how to assist clients with diverse needs can enhance the experience for all participants and create a welcoming atmosphere.

Incorporating nutritional meal prep services into fitness programs can also enhance inclusivity. Entrepreneurs should consider dietary restrictions and preferences when designing meal plans, ensuring that options are available for individuals with allergies, vegan or vegetarian diets, and other nutritional needs. By collaborating with nutritionists and dietitians, wellness franchises can create comprehensive programs that address the diverse dietary requirements of their clientele, promoting better overall health and wellness.

Another critical aspect of creating inclusive fitness programs is the implementation of technology and online platforms. With the rise of virtual training and fitness apps, wellness businesses can reach a broader audience by offering online classes and resources tailored to various fitness levels and abilities. This not only allows for flexibility but also provides an opportunity for individuals who may feel intimidated by traditional gym environments to engage in fitness at their own pace and comfort level.

Lastly, fostering community engagement through wellness retreats and specialized classes can build a sense of belonging among participants. By organizing events that celebrate diversity and encourage participation from all community members, fitness entrepreneurs can create spaces where everyone feels valued and motivated to pursue their health goals. Emphasizing mental health and wellness coaching within these programs further supports participants in their overall journey, promoting a holistic approach to health that considers both physical and emotional well-being. In doing so, businesses can position themselves as leaders in the wellness industry, driving success through inclusivity and community connection.

Marketing Specialized Classes to Target Audiences

Marketing specialized classes to target audiences is essential for maximizing engagement and ensuring the sustainability of health and wellness franchises. Entrepreneurs looking to thrive in this competitive landscape must understand the unique needs of their target demographics. In a world where personalization is increasingly demanded, tailoring marketing strategies to specific audiences can significantly enhance the effectiveness of outreach efforts. By identifying niche markets, entrepreneurs can create specialized classes that resonate with potential clients, ultimately driving memberships and participation.

One effective approach to market specialized classes is to leverage demographic insights and psychographics. Understanding the specific characteristics, preferences, and challenges of your target audience is crucial. For instance, yoga for seniors requires different marketing strategies compared to high-intensity interval training (HIIT) classes aimed at younger adults. Creating targeted messaging that speaks directly to the values and lifestyle of each group can foster a stronger connection. Utilizing data from surveys and market research can provide valuable insights into what motivates potential clients, enabling franchises to develop offerings that meet their needs.

Digital marketing plays a pivotal role in reaching specialized audiences. Social media platforms, email marketing, and targeted online advertising can be powerful tools for promoting classes. For instance, wellness retreats can be marketed through visually appealing content showcasing serene environments and testimonials from past participants. Additionally, partnerships with local influencers in the wellness space can amplify reach and credibility. Entrepreneurs should also consider creating valuable content, such as blogs or videos, that speaks to the interests of their target audience, positioning their brand as an authority in the wellness sector.

Community engagement is another critical element of marketing specialized classes. Hosting free introductory sessions or workshops can attract potential clients and allow them to experience the benefits of the classes firsthand. Collaborating with local health practitioners, nutritionists, or mental health coaches can enhance credibility and broaden the appeal of offerings. Networking within the community not only fosters relationships but also creates word-of-mouth marketing, which is invaluable in the health and wellness industry. Entrepreneurs should actively participate in local events and health fairs to promote their specialized classes and connect with potential clients.

Finally, measuring the effectiveness of marketing efforts is essential for continuous improvement. Franchise owners should utilize analytics tools to track engagement, conversion rates, and customer feedback. This data can inform future marketing strategies and help refine class offerings to better meet the evolving needs of the target audience. By adopting a proactive approach to marketing specialized classes, entrepreneurs can ensure their health and wellness franchises not only attract clients but also cultivate a loyal and engaged community, ultimately leading to long-term success in the industry.

11

Chapter 11: Health-Focused Meal Delivery Franchises

The Intersection of Convenience and Health

The intersection of convenience and health represents a dynamic and evolving landscape within the wellness industry, particularly as consumers increasingly seek solutions that seamlessly integrate into their busy lifestyles. For entrepreneurs and franchise owners, understanding this intersection is crucial to developing services and products that resonate with health-conscious consumers. The rise of mobile fitness studios, nutritional meal prep services, and online personal training platforms exemplifies the demand for accessible health and wellness options. These innovations not only simplify the process of maintaining a healthy lifestyle but also cater to a diverse clientele seeking flexibility without compromising their well-being.

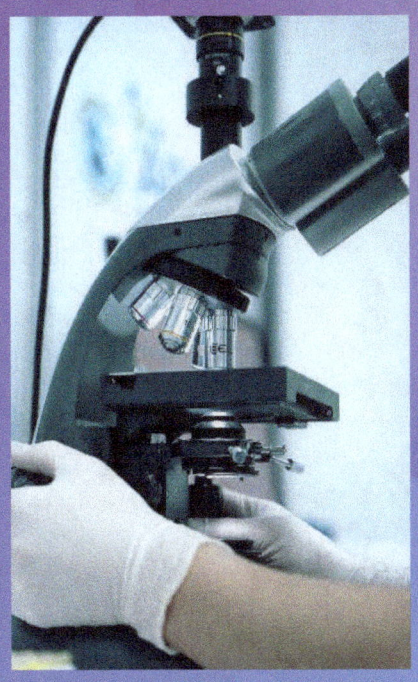

One of the primary drivers of this trend is the growing emphasis on convenience in daily routines. As consumers juggle work, family, and personal commitments, they are often left with limited time to dedicate to their health. Franchises that offer health-focused meal delivery services or corporate wellness programs capitalize on this need by providing tailored solutions that fit into busy schedules.

By leveraging technology, such as mobile apps for scheduling workouts or tracking nutrition, businesses can create a more user-friendly experience that encourages engagement and fosters a sense of community among clients.

Moreover, specialized fitness classes, such as yoga for seniors or mental health and wellness coaching, highlight the importance of accessibility in health and fitness. These programs not only cater to specific demographics but also emphasize the need for inclusive offerings that accommodate varying levels of ability and interest. Entrepreneurs can thrive by recognizing the diverse needs of their target market and developing franchises that prioritize both convenience and health, thereby fostering a supportive environment for all participants.

The rise of eco-friendly fitness products and wellness retreats further illustrates the intersection of convenience and health, as consumers become increasingly mindful of their choices' broader impact. Sustainable practices attract a growing segment of the population that values not just personal health but also environmental well-being. By aligning their business models with eco-conscious principles, franchise owners can appeal to this demographic while contributing to a healthier planet, creating a win-win situation that enhances brand loyalty and market reach.

In conclusion, the intersection of convenience and health presents a wealth of opportunities for entrepreneurs in the wellness industry. By embracing innovative solutions that prioritize accessibility and sustainability, franchise owners can build successful businesses that not only meet consumer demands but also contribute positively to the communities they serve. As the health and fitness landscape continues to evolve, those who adapt and respond to these trends will undoubtedly lead the charge in the Fit Franchise Revolution.

Building a Scalable Meal Delivery Model

Building a scalable meal delivery model requires a comprehensive understanding of the health and wellness market, along with the ability to adapt to consumer demands. Entrepreneurs venturing into this space must first identify their target demographic, whether it be fitness enthusiasts, busy professionals, or families seeking healthier meal options. By conducting thorough market research and analyzing current trends, business owners can create meal plans that align with the nutritional needs and preferences of their audience. This foundational research informs not just the menu but also the branding and marketing strategies that will resonate with potential customers.

Once the target market is established, developing a streamlined operational framework is essential for scalability. A successful meal delivery service must have efficient systems for sourcing ingredients, preparing meals, packaging, and distributing them. Utilizing technology is crucial here; implementing an inventory management system can help keep track of supplies while a robust logistics plan ensures timely deliveries. Investing in training staff to uphold quality and consistency across all locations or franchises will further solidify the brand's reputation and customer satisfaction, which are vital for growth.

Sustainability plays a significant role in the modern consumer's decision-making process, particularly within the health-conscious segment. Incorporating eco-friendly practices not only reduces environmental impact but also attracts a loyal customer base that values corporate responsibility. From using biodegradable packaging to sourcing locally grown, organic ingredients, entrepreneurs can differentiate their services in a saturated market. Moreover, highlighting these sustainable practices in marketing campaigns can enhance brand image and appeal to a broader audience, including those who prioritize wellness and environmental consciousness.

Scalability also hinges on the ability to adapt the business model to different markets and locations. Franchise opportunities can be an effective way to expand reach without sacrificing quality or brand identity. By providing franchisees with a comprehensive training program, operational guidelines, and marketing support, the business can maintain consistency while empowering local entrepreneurs. This approach not only accelerates growth but also fosters community engagement, as franchisees often have a vested interest in the neighborhoods they serve.

Finally, leveraging technology for customer engagement and feedback can significantly enhance the meal delivery model. Implementing a user-friendly app or website allows customers to customize their meal plans, schedule deliveries, and provide feedback on their experience. Data analytics can be utilized to track preferences and purchasing patterns, enabling continuous improvement of the service. By fostering a two-way communication channel, businesses can build lasting relationships with their customers, ensuring loyalty and sustained growth in the competitive landscape of health-focused meal delivery services.

Challenges in the Meal Delivery Space

The meal delivery space has seen explosive growth in recent years, particularly in the health and wellness sector. However, entrepreneurs and franchise owners face a unique set of challenges that can hinder their success. One of the primary issues is the highly competitive nature of the market. With numerous players vying for consumer attention, distinguishing a brand becomes crucial. Companies must not only offer high-quality, nutritious meals but also develop a compelling brand story and unique selling proposition that resonates with health-conscious consumers. Another significant challenge is the logistics of food delivery. Ensuring that meals remain fresh, nutritious, and appealing during transit requires efficient supply chain management. This includes sourcing high-quality ingredients, managing inventory, and maintaining optimal storage conditions. Additionally, meal delivery services must navigate the complexities of food safety regulations, which can vary by region. Entrepreneurs must invest in knowledgeable staff and reliable systems to handle food preparation and delivery while adhering to health standards.

Consumer trends also present challenges in the meal delivery space. As preferences shift toward plant-based, organic, or allergen-free options, businesses must remain adaptable. Entrepreneurs need to stay informed about dietary trends and consumer demands to adjust their menus accordingly. This necessity for flexibility can strain resources, as developing new recipes and sourcing varied ingredients can be time-consuming and costly. Failure to adapt to these evolving preferences can lead to customer dissatisfaction and lost revenue.

Customer retention is another hurdle in this sector. While attracting new clients is essential, maintaining existing relationships is equally important. Meal delivery services often face high churn rates, as consumers may experiment with different options or revert to home cooking. To combat this, businesses must prioritize exceptional customer service, offer loyalty programs, and solicit feedback to improve their offerings continually. Engaging customers through social media and personalized marketing can help cultivate a loyal community around the brand. Lastly, the integration of technology in meal delivery poses both opportunities and challenges. While digital platforms can streamline ordering and payment processes, they also require significant investment in software development and cybersecurity. Additionally, as consumers increasingly rely on mobile apps and websites for their meal choices, ensuring a seamless user experience becomes vital. Entrepreneurs must balance the benefits of technology with the potential risks associated with data privacy and system reliability, making informed decisions about their digital strategies.

Chapter 12: Fitness Technology and Wearable Devices

The Role of Technology in Fitness

The role of technology in fitness has transformed the landscape of health and wellness, creating new opportunities for entrepreneurs and businesses to leverage. With advancements in digital platforms and mobile applications, fitness solutions have become more accessible and personalized. Entrepreneurs in the wellness industry can now harness these technologies to meet the evolving demands of consumers who seek convenience, engagement, and tailored experiences. From mobile fitness studios to online personal training, technology enables businesses to reach broader audiences and enhance customer satisfaction.

Wearable devices have emerged as a significant trend within the fitness sector, allowing individuals to monitor their health metrics in real time. These devices track various parameters such as heart rate, calories burned, and even sleep patterns, providing users with actionable insights to improve their fitness journey. For entrepreneurs, integrating wearable technology into their offerings can add value to their services and create a more comprehensive wellness experience. Franchises can differentiate themselves by incorporating these technologies, appealing to health-conscious consumers who are increasingly reliant on data-driven approaches to fitness.

Moreover, the rise of virtual training platforms has revolutionized the way fitness services are delivered. Entrepreneurs can capitalize on this trend by establishing online personal training platforms that allow clients to engage with fitness professionals remotely. This model not only reduces overhead costs associated with physical locations but also expands market reach, enabling businesses to cater to clients who prefer the convenience of home workouts. By offering flexible scheduling and personalized programs through technology, wellness businesses can enhance client retention and satisfaction.

In addition to fitness training, technology plays a vital role in nutritional meal prep and delivery services. Health-focused meal delivery franchises can utilize apps and online platforms to streamline ordering processes and tailor meal plans based on individual dietary needs and preferences. This integration of technology ensures that customers receive not only nutritious meals but also a seamless experience from selection to delivery. Entrepreneurs who embrace such innovations position themselves at the forefront of the health and wellness industry, meeting the growing demand for convenient and healthy eating options.

Lastly, technology also enhances corporate wellness programs by providing tools for engagement and accountability. Businesses can implement platforms that offer wellness challenges, health assessments, and progress tracking to encourage employee participation and foster a culture of health. By leveraging technology, franchises can deliver customized wellness solutions that meet the specific needs of corporate clients, ultimately leading to improved employee well-being and productivity. The integration of technology in fitness is not just a trend; it is a fundamental shift that presents significant opportunities for entrepreneurs in the health and wellness space to innovate and thrive.

Staying Ahead with Wearable Innovations

Wearable innovations are transforming the landscape of health and wellness, offering entrepreneurs and franchise operators the tools necessary to stay competitive in an ever-evolving market. These devices, ranging from fitness trackers to smart clothing, not only enhance personal health management but also provide actionable insights that can be leveraged for business growth. By integrating wearable technology into their offerings, franchise owners can optimize customer engagement, tailor experiences, and improve overall service quality, thus positioning themselves at the forefront of the industry.

The rise of wearable devices has made it easier for individuals to monitor their physical activity, sleep patterns, and even stress levels. For franchise businesses, this presents an opportunity to create personalized fitness programs that cater to the specific needs of their clients. For instance, mobile fitness studios can incorporate wearable technology to track clients' progress in real-time, enabling trainers to adjust workouts based on individual performance and goals. This level of customization fosters loyalty and encourages clients to remain committed to their health journey, which is essential for franchise success.

Moreover, the data generated by wearables can inform marketing strategies and operational decisions. Entrepreneurs in the health and wellness sector can utilize analytics from wearable devices to identify trends and preferences among their client base. This insight allows for the development of targeted promotional campaigns, specialized classes, and tailored wellness retreats that resonate with customers. By understanding what motivates their audience, franchise owners can enhance the effectiveness of their offerings and create a more compelling value proposition.

In the realm of corporate wellness programs, wearables offer significant benefits as well. Businesses are increasingly looking for ways to improve employee health and productivity, and incorporating wearable technology into wellness initiatives can facilitate this goal. By providing employees with fitness trackers and encouraging friendly competition through challenges, companies can promote a culture of health that not only boosts morale but also reduces healthcare costs. For entrepreneurs in the corporate wellness space, this trend represents a lucrative avenue for franchise development and partnership opportunities.

As the health and wellness industry continues to evolve, staying ahead with wearable innovations is crucial for franchise success. By embracing these technologies, entrepreneurs can enhance their service offerings, foster stronger client relationships, and ultimately drive profitability. The integration of wearables into business models is not just a trend; it is a strategic imperative that will define the future of fitness and wellness franchising. As more consumers prioritize their health and seek innovative solutions, those who adapt and leverage wearable technology will emerge as leaders in this dynamic industry.

Integrating Technology into Franchise Operations

Integrating technology into franchise operations is a pivotal strategy for enhancing efficiency, improving customer engagement, and streamlining service delivery in the health and wellness industry. Franchises can leverage various technological innovations, from mobile applications to wearable devices, to create a seamless experience for both franchise owners and customers. By adopting these technologies, franchises not only stay competitive but also meet the evolving expectations of tech-savvy consumers who value accessibility and personalization in their health and wellness journeys.

Mobile fitness studios can particularly benefit from technology integration by utilizing apps that facilitate scheduling, client management, and payment processing. These applications enable trainers to connect directly with clients, providing instant updates about classes, promotions, and personalized fitness plans. By employing geolocation services, mobile studios can also target specific demographics in various locations, optimizing their marketing efforts and improving customer acquisition rates. The ability to track customer engagement through these platforms allows franchise owners to make data-driven decisions that enhance service offerings and drive growth.

In the realm of nutritional meal prep services, technology plays a crucial role in inventory management and meal customization. Franchises can implement software that tracks ingredient availability, helps in menu planning, and analyzes customer preferences. This integration not only minimizes food waste but also ensures that meals are tailored to the dietary needs of clients. Additionally, the use of online ordering systems and delivery apps enhances convenience, allowing customers to easily access healthy meal options while providing valuable insights into consumer behavior for franchise owners.

Wellness retreats and getaway franchises can enrich their offerings by incorporating virtual reality (VR) and augmented reality (AR) technologies. These tools can enhance the client experience by providing immersive environments for relaxation and meditation practices, making retreats more attractive to potential clients. Furthermore, adopting online platforms for pre-retreat engagement, such as webinars or virtual tours, allows franchises to build excitement and connection with customers before they arrive. This proactive approach not only fosters loyalty but also sets the stage for a more personalized experience during the retreat.

Finally, the integration of fitness technology and wearable devices into corporate wellness programs is becoming increasingly relevant. These devices can track physical activity, stress levels, and overall health metrics, providing valuable data that can be used to tailor wellness initiatives to meet the specific needs of employees. By partnering with tech companies to offer discounts on wearable devices or fitness apps, franchises can enhance their appeal to corporate clients. This tech-forward approach not only positions the franchise as a leader in the wellness industry but also demonstrates a commitment to promoting health and well-being in the workplace, ultimately leading to higher employee satisfaction and productivity.

Chapter 13: Building a Successful Franchise

Essential Steps to Franchise Development

Franchise development in the health and wellness sector requires a strategic approach that aligns with the unique needs of this industry. The first essential step is conducting thorough market research. This involves understanding current trends, identifying target demographics, and assessing the competitive landscape. Entrepreneurs must analyze consumer preferences and behaviors related to health and wellness, as well as emerging niches such as mobile fitness studios or online personal training platforms. Gathering data on regional health statistics and wellness interests can provide valuable insights that inform franchise offerings and positioning.

Once market research is complete, the next step is to create a robust business model that clearly defines the franchise's value proposition. This model should outline the services or products offered, pricing strategies, and operational frameworks that can be replicated across multiple locations. For example, a nutritional meal prep service must consider sourcing ingredients, meal customization options, and delivery logistics. Establishing a strong brand identity that resonates with health-conscious consumers is crucial, as it will differentiate the franchise in a crowded market.

After solidifying the business model, potential franchisors should develop comprehensive operational procedures and training programs. This includes creating detailed manuals that cover everything from marketing strategies to staff training and customer service protocols. In the wellness industry, where personal interaction and customer satisfaction are paramount, ensuring that franchisees are well-equipped to uphold the brand's standards is essential. Offering continuous support and resources, such as workshops and access to industry experts, can help franchisees thrive in their local markets.

Legal considerations are another critical component of franchise development. It is vital to draft a Franchise Disclosure Document (FDD) that complies with federal and state regulations. This document must transparently outline the franchise's financial performance, fees, and obligations, protecting both the franchisor and franchisees. Consulting with legal professionals who specialize in franchising and the health and wellness industry can ensure that all necessary legal frameworks are in place, minimizing potential disputes down the line.

Finally, the launch phase of franchise development requires a well-planned marketing strategy to attract potential franchisees and customers. Utilizing digital marketing tools, social media platforms, and community engagement initiatives can effectively build brand awareness and attract a loyal customer base. For franchises focused on eco-friendly fitness products or specialized fitness classes, showcasing unique selling points through targeted campaigns can further enhance visibility. The success of a franchise in the health and wellness sector hinges not just on the quality of its offerings but also on the strength of its brand presence in a competitive landscape.

Legal and Financial Considerations

When venturing into the health and wellness franchise sector, understanding the legal landscape is paramount for entrepreneurs. Franchising is governed by a complex web of federal and state regulations. Franchise agreements typically outline the rights and responsibilities of both the franchisor and the franchisee, including operational protocols, intellectual property usage, and termination clauses. Entrepreneurs must ensure that they are compliant with the Franchise Disclosure Document (FDD), which provides critical information about the franchise system, including fees, obligations, and the franchisor's financial performance. Engaging with a legal expert familiar with franchise law can help navigate these requirements and avoid potential pitfalls.

Financial considerations play a crucial role in the success of a franchise. Initial investment costs can vary widely across different niches in the health and wellness industry, from mobile fitness studios to nutritional meal prep services. Entrepreneurs must conduct thorough due diligence to understand not only the franchise fees but also ongoing royalty payments, marketing contributions, and unexpected expenses. Creating a comprehensive financial plan that includes projected revenue, operating costs, and potential funding sources is essential. This plan will serve as a roadmap for the franchise's financial health and can be instrumental when seeking financing from banks or investors.

Securing financing is often one of the first steps for aspiring franchise owners. There are several options available, including traditional bank loans, Small Business Administration (SBA) loans, and alternative funding sources such as crowdfunding or private investors. Each option comes with its own set of advantages and disadvantages, particularly in terms of interest rates, repayment terms, and the level of control retained by the entrepreneur. Understanding these financial instruments and selecting the right one based on personal financial circumstances and business goals can greatly impact the long-term sustainability of the franchise.

Moreover, when establishing a franchise, it is imperative to consider the ongoing financial obligations that come with running a business in the wellness sector. This includes not only the costs associated with inventory, equipment, and rent but also the expenses tied to marketing and customer acquisition. Entrepreneurs should also factor in the costs of compliance with health and safety regulations, which can be particularly stringent in wellness-related franchises. By forecasting these expenses and incorporating them into the business model, franchisees can better manage cash flow and ensure that their franchise remains profitable.

Lastly, the importance of protecting intellectual property cannot be overstated in the health and wellness franchise industry. Whether it's branding, proprietary training methods, or unique product formulas, safeguarding these assets is essential for maintaining competitive advantage. Entrepreneurs should consider registering trademarks and copyrights as necessary, and should remain vigilant against potential infringements. By implementing robust legal protections and regularly reviewing compliance standards, franchise owners can foster a thriving business environment that not only attracts customers but also builds a reputable brand in the health and wellness space.

Creating a Supportive Franchise Network

Creating a supportive franchise network is essential for the success of any franchise in the health and wellness industry. This network serves as the backbone for franchisees, providing them with the resources, knowledge, and community necessary to thrive. A well-structured support system can enhance the operational efficiency of each franchise unit while promoting a cohesive brand identity. Understanding the unique challenges faced by franchisees in sectors such as mobile fitness studios, nutritional meal prep services, and wellness retreats is crucial for developing tailored support strategies.

Effective communication is a cornerstone of a supportive franchise network. Franchise systems must establish clear channels for sharing information and resources among franchisees. Regular updates on best practices, marketing strategies, and operational efficiencies can empower franchisees to make informed decisions. Utilizing technology, such as dedicated online platforms or mobile apps, can facilitate real-time communication and collaboration. This ensures that franchisees remain engaged and informed, allowing them to adapt to industry trends and consumer demands swiftly.

Training and development programs are another critical component of a supportive franchise network. Providing comprehensive onboarding for new franchisees helps them understand the brand's values and operational standards. Ongoing education opportunities, such as workshops, webinars, and certification programs, can further enhance the skills of franchisees and their staff. For instance, specialized training in mental health coaching or eco-friendly fitness products can equip franchisees with the expertise needed to meet the diverse needs of their customer base, ultimately driving customer satisfaction and loyalty.

A sense of community can significantly impact a franchise network's overall morale and performance. Developing a culture of collaboration among franchisees fosters relationships that extend beyond business transactions. Organizing annual conventions, regional meetups, or online forums can create opportunities for franchisees to share their experiences, challenges, and successes. This camaraderie can lead to valuable partnerships, mentorship opportunities, and the exchange of innovative ideas, ultimately contributing to the growth and resilience of the franchise as a whole.

Lastly, recognizing and celebrating franchisee achievements is vital for reinforcing a supportive network. Acknowledging milestones, such as sales targets or successful marketing campaigns, can motivate franchisees to pursue excellence. Implementing reward systems or recognition programs can enhance franchisee engagement and loyalty to the brand. By fostering an environment where franchisees feel valued and appreciated, the franchise network can cultivate a strong sense of belonging, which is essential for long-term success in the competitive health and wellness sector.

Chapter 14: Marketing Your Health and Wellness Franchise

Branding Strategies for Wellness Franchises

Branding strategies for wellness franchises are critical in establishing a strong market presence and differentiating services in a competitive landscape. A well-crafted brand communicates the core values and mission of the franchise, resonating with the target audience's desire for health and wellness. For entrepreneurs venturing into health and fitness, it is essential to define a unique brand identity that reflects the benefits of their offerings, whether that involves innovative fitness technology, eco-friendly products, or specialized wellness programs. By focusing on authenticity and clarity in messaging, franchises can create a memorable impression that attracts and retains customers.

One effective branding strategy is to leverage storytelling to connect with potential clients on an emotional level. Sharing the journey that inspired the creation of the franchise can foster a sense of community and shared purpose. For instance, a mobile fitness studio could narrate how it started as a response to the lack of accessible fitness options in certain neighborhoods. Wellness retreats, on the other hand, might highlight transformative personal experiences that showcase the benefits of their services. This narrative approach not only humanizes the brand but also encourages customer loyalty by inviting them to be part of a larger mission.
Another crucial aspect of branding is visual identity. The choice of colors, logos, and design elements should align with the wellness ethos of the franchise. For example, brands focused on mental health and wellness coaching might opt for calming colors and minimalist designs that evoke tranquility and trust. Fitness technology and wearable devices could incorporate sleek, modern aesthetics that communicate innovation and functionality. Consistency across all marketing materials, from social media to packaging, reinforces brand recognition and ensures that the franchise stands out in a crowded marketplace.
Engaging in community-building initiatives is also a powerful branding strategy for wellness franchises. By hosting local events, workshops, or free classes, franchises can create a platform for interactions that foster relationships with potential customers. For instance, a nutritional meal prep service could offer cooking classes that not only showcase their products but also educate participants on healthy eating habits. This hands-on engagement not only enhances brand visibility but also positions the franchise as a valuable resource in the health and wellness community, ultimately driving customer acquisition and retention.
Finally, incorporating customer feedback into branding strategies can significantly enhance brand credibility. Encouraging clients to share their testimonials, success stories, or even challenges creates a sense of ownership and trust in the brand. For wellness retreats and getaway franchises, showcasing guest experiences through reviews and social media content can serve as powerful endorsements. Additionally, responding to feedback and demonstrating a commitment to continuous improvement reinforces the brand's dedication to customer satisfaction and well-being. In the rapidly evolving world of wellness franchises, adapting branding strategies based on real customer insights can lead to sustained growth and a loyal customer base.

Digital Marketing Tactics

Digital marketing has become an essential tool for entrepreneurs in the health and wellness industry, particularly for those operating within franchise models. The unique nature of health and wellness franchises demands targeted digital marketing tactics that resonate with a diverse audience. Building brand awareness and attracting potential clients through effective online strategies can significantly influence the success of a franchise. By utilizing various digital platforms, businesses can engage with customers, promote their services, and drive growth in a competitive market.

One effective tactic is leveraging social media platforms to build community and foster engagement. Health and wellness brands can create tailored content that appeals to their target demographics, such as success stories, workout tips, or healthy recipes. Platforms like Instagram and Facebook are particularly effective for visually driven content that showcases fitness classes, meal prep services, or wellness retreats. Regular interaction through comments, shares, and direct messaging can help establish a loyal customer base, making social media a powerful tool for franchise owners looking to enhance their visibility.

Search engine optimization (SEO) is another crucial tactic for driving organic traffic to health and wellness franchise websites. By optimizing their online content with relevant keywords, businesses can improve their search engine rankings and increase visibility to potential clients searching for specific services, such as online personal training or corporate wellness programs. High-quality blog posts, informative articles, and resourceful guides can enhance credibility while addressing common queries related to health and fitness. This tactic not only helps in acquiring new leads but also positions the franchise as a thought leader in the wellness space.

Email marketing remains a reliable strategy for maintaining customer relationships and driving repeat business. By building an email list through promotions, newsletters, and valuable content, health and wellness franchises can communicate directly with clients. Personalized emails can inform subscribers about new classes, upcoming wellness retreats, or special promotions on fitness technology products. This tactic allows businesses to nurture leads and encourage existing clients to engage with new offerings, ultimately fostering loyalty and community.

Lastly, utilizing paid advertising can provide a significant boost to digital marketing efforts. Platforms like Google Ads and social media ads allow franchises to target specific demographics interested in health and wellness. By investing in pay-per-click campaigns or sponsored posts, business owners can reach a wider audience and generate leads more quickly. Targeted ads can be particularly effective for niche offerings, such as eco-friendly fitness products or specialized fitness classes, ensuring that the right message reaches the right audience at the right time. By combining these digital marketing tactics, entrepreneurs in the health and wellness sector can build a strong online presence and drive their franchise success.

Building Community and Engagement

Building a strong community and fostering engagement are essential components in the success of any health and wellness franchise. Entrepreneurs in this sector must recognize that their businesses extend beyond mere transactions; they are part of a larger lifestyle movement. Creating a sense of belonging among customers not only enhances loyalty but also transforms patrons into advocates for the brand. This can be achieved through various strategies that encourage interaction, participation, and a shared commitment to health and wellness.

One effective way to build community is by hosting regular events that cater to the interests of your clientele. These can range from fitness classes and health workshops to wellness retreats and nutritional meal prep demonstrations. By offering diverse experiences, franchises can engage various demographics within the health and wellness sphere. For instance, a mobile fitness studio might organize pop-up classes in local parks, while a nutritional meal prep service could host cooking demonstrations at community centers. These events not only promote the brand but also create opportunities for participants to connect with each other, fostering relationships that extend beyond the initial engagement.

Utilizing digital platforms is another key strategy for enhancing community and engagement. Online personal training platforms can leverage social media to create interactive content, such as live-streamed workouts, health challenges, and educational webinars. This not only provides value to existing clients but also attracts new participants who are looking for a sense of community in their fitness journey. Moreover, implementing forums or chat groups within these platforms allows clients to share experiences, advice, and encouragement, further solidifying their connection to the brand and to each other.

Incorporating feedback mechanisms is vital for maintaining engagement and ensuring the community feels heard. Regular surveys and polls can provide valuable insights into customer preferences and areas for improvement. This not only demonstrates that the franchise values its members' opinions but also helps shape offerings that truly resonate with the audience. For specialized fitness classes, such as yoga for seniors or corporate wellness programs, understanding the specific needs of these groups can lead to tailored services that enhance satisfaction and retention.

Finally, collaboration with like-minded businesses and organizations can amplify community-building efforts. Partnering with local health food stores, mental health coaches, or eco-friendly fitness product companies can create a network of support that benefits all parties involved. Joint events or promotional campaigns can help reach a broader audience, while also reinforcing the commitment to holistic health and wellness. By fostering collaborations, franchises can enhance their visibility and credibility, ultimately creating a vibrant community that thrives on shared values and goals.

Chapter 15: Future of the Fit Franchise Revolution

Predictions for the Health and Wellness Industry

The health and wellness industry is poised for transformative growth in the coming years, driven by evolving consumer preferences and advancements in technology. Entrepreneurs and franchise owners should anticipate a surge in demand for personalized health solutions, reflecting a broader societal shift towards holistic well-being. As consumers increasingly prioritize their health, services that combine fitness, nutrition, and mental wellness will become essential, creating lucrative opportunities for those in the industry. This trend will likely lead to the emergence of new franchise models that cater to individualized wellness journeys, blending mobile fitness studios with nutritional meal prep services for a comprehensive approach.

Another significant development on the horizon is the expansion of online platforms for personal training and health coaching. The pandemic accelerated the adoption of digital fitness solutions, and this trend is expected to continue. Entrepreneurs should explore the potential of hybrid models that integrate virtual services with in-person experiences. Online personal training platforms that offer tailored programs and real-time feedback will resonate with consumers seeking convenience and flexibility. Additionally, corporate wellness programs will likely see increased investment as businesses recognize the importance of employee well-being in enhancing productivity and morale.

Moreover, eco-friendly fitness products and practices are emerging as a critical niche within the health and wellness landscape. Consumers are becoming more environmentally conscious, seeking products that align with their values. This shift presents an opportunity for franchises that prioritize sustainability, such as eco-friendly gyms or wellness retreats that utilize natural resources efficiently. By aligning business practices with sustainability, entrepreneurs can attract a dedicated customer base that is committed to supporting eco-conscious brands.

The trend toward specialized fitness classes, such as yoga for seniors or high-intensity interval training (HIIT) for busy professionals, is also expected to grow. As the population ages, there will be an increasing demand for fitness offerings tailored to specific demographics and health needs. Franchises that focus on inclusivity and cater to diverse age groups and fitness levels will likely thrive. By offering specialized programs, franchise owners can differentiate themselves in a competitive market and build strong community ties.

Finally, the integration of fitness technology and wearable devices will continue to shape the industry. As consumers become more data-driven in their health journeys, businesses that leverage technology to enhance user experience will have a competitive edge. Wearable fitness trackers, mobile apps for tracking nutrition and workouts, and virtual coaching platforms will become essential tools for both consumers and franchise operators. Entrepreneurs who harness these technologies to provide actionable insights and personalized recommendations will not only improve client satisfaction but also drive business growth in an increasingly tech-savvy market.

Adapting to Changing Consumer Preferences

Adapting to changing consumer preferences is essential for entrepreneurs and franchise operators in the health and wellness industry. As societal norms shift and awareness of health issues grows, consumer expectations evolve, demanding innovations that align with their lifestyles. Understanding these preferences allows businesses to tailor their offerings more effectively, ensuring they remain relevant and competitive. This adaptation is not merely a response to trends but a proactive strategy to cultivate loyalty and meet the diverse needs of a broad customer base.

One significant shift in consumer preferences is the increasing demand for convenience. Busy lifestyles have led many individuals to seek accessible health and fitness solutions that fit seamlessly into their daily routines. Mobile fitness studios and online personal training platforms have gained popularity, as they provide flexibility and affordability without compromising on quality. Entrepreneurs must recognize this shift and explore opportunities to integrate technology into their business models, such as offering app-based scheduling for classes or providing virtual coaching options to meet clients where they are.

Another critical aspect of adapting to changing consumer preferences is the growing focus on holistic wellness. Today's consumers view health as a multifaceted concept that encompasses physical fitness, mental well-being, nutrition, and lifestyle choices. This holistic approach has spurred the rise of wellness retreats, nutritional meal prep services, and corporate wellness programs that prioritize comprehensive health strategies. Entrepreneurs should consider diversifying their services to include mental health coaching and eco-friendly products, tapping into the increasing consumer desire for sustainable and ethically sourced options.

The rise of specialized fitness classes also highlights changing consumer preferences. As more individuals seek tailored experiences that cater to their unique needs, niche markets such as yoga for seniors and fitness programs for specific health conditions are thriving. Franchise operators can capitalize on this trend by developing specialized offerings that appeal to targeted demographics. By conducting market research and engaging with potential clients, entrepreneurs can identify gaps in the market and create programs that resonate with specific audiences, enhancing their competitive edge.

Finally, leveraging fitness technology and wearable devices is a vital component in adapting to consumer preferences. Today's consumers are tech-savvy and often seek tools that enhance their fitness journey, from tracking progress to providing personalized insights. Integrating technology into fitness programs not only improves client engagement but also fosters a sense of community through shared experiences and challenges. Entrepreneurs should stay informed about technological advancements and consider partnerships with tech companies to create innovative solutions that elevate their services, ultimately driving success in the ever-evolving health and wellness landscape.

The Ongoing Journey of Franchise Innovation

The ongoing journey of franchise innovation in the health and wellness sector is a dynamic process that continuously adapts to the changing needs and preferences of consumers. In recent years, franchise models have evolved to incorporate new technologies, personalized services, and unique experiences that enhance customer engagement. Entrepreneurs in this space are not only responding to market demands but are also setting trends that redefine how health and wellness services are delivered. This innovation-driven approach is integral to fostering long-term success in the competitive landscape of health and wellness franchising. One notable trend in franchise innovation is the rise of mobile fitness studios, which cater to a growing demand for convenience and flexibility. These franchises capitalize on the busy lifestyles of modern consumers by bringing fitness directly to their neighborhoods, workplaces, or even homes. By utilizing innovative scheduling platforms and engaging marketing strategies, mobile fitness studios have become a viable option for those who may find traditional gym environments intimidating or inconvenient. This adaptability not only attracts a broader audience but also creates an opportunity for franchise owners to tap into diverse revenue streams.

Nutritional meal prep services have also emerged as a significant player in the franchise landscape, emphasizing the importance of healthy eating in achieving wellness goals. The integration of meal planning with fitness regimens allows franchisees to offer comprehensive solutions that meet the nutritional needs of their clients. Innovative meal prep franchises are leveraging technology, such as app-based ordering systems and personalized meal plans, to enhance user experience and streamline operations. As consumers increasingly seek convenience and health-conscious options, these franchises are positioned to thrive in the evolving market.

Wellness retreats and getaway franchises represent another facet of the ongoing journey of franchise innovation. These establishments provide immersive experiences that focus on holistic health, combining fitness, nutrition, and mental well-being. Franchise owners are embracing sustainable practices and eco-friendly initiatives, aligning their offerings with the values of environmentally conscious consumers. By creating unique and rejuvenating experiences, wellness retreats not only attract clients seeking relaxation and rejuvenation but also promote the importance of mental health and self-care in today's fast-paced world.

The rise of online personal training platforms highlights the importance of accessibility and community in wellness franchising. These platforms allow trainers to reach clients beyond geographical limitations, offering tailored fitness programs that cater to individual needs. Additionally, the integration of fitness technology and wearable devices has revolutionized how consumers track their progress and engage with their wellness journeys. Franchisees who embrace these technological advancements can create a more interactive and supportive environment that encourages client retention and satisfaction. As the health and wellness industry continues to innovate, the potential for franchise success remains vast, driven by the commitment to meeting the evolving demands of consumers.

www.ingramcontent.com/pod-product-compliance
Lightning Source LLC
Chambersburg PA
CBHW070202230526
45471CB00002B/784